3 4028 07206 5361
HARRIS COUNTY PUBLIC LIBRARY

248.4 Hal
Hall, Mark, 1969-
Your own Jesus : a God insistent on
making it personal /
$16.99   ocn318057907

WITHDRAWN

D1112472

YOUR OWN JESUS

A God Insistent on Making It Personal

MARK HALL

WITH TIM LUKE

ZONDERVAN®

ZONDERVAN.com/
AUTHORTRACKER
follow your favorite authors

ZONDERVAN

Your Own Jesus
Copyright © 2009 by Mark Hall

This title is also available as a Zondervan ebook.
Visit www.zondervan.com/ebooks.

This title is also available in a Zondervan audio edition.
Visit www.zondervan.fm.

Requests for information should be addressed to:

Zondervan, *Grand Rapids, Michigan 49530*

Library of Congress Cataloging-in-Publication Data

Hall, Mark, 1970 –
    Your own Jesus : a God insistent on making it personal / Mark Hall with
  Tim Luke.
        p.   cm.
     ISBN 978-0-310-29332-3 (hardcover)
     1. Christian life — Baptist authors. I. Luke, Tim. II. Title.
  BV4501.3.H3483   2009
    248.4 — dc22   2009014020

All Scripture quotations, unless otherwise indicated, are taken from *The Holy Bible, English Standard Version*, copyright © 2001 by Crossway Bibles, a division of Good News Publishers. Used by permission. All rights reserved.

Scripture quotations marked NKJV are taken from the New King James Version. Copyright © 1982, by Thomas Nelson, Inc. Used by permission. All rights reserved.

Scripture quotations marked NIV are taken from *The Holy Bible, New International Version*®. NIV®. Copyright © 1973, 1978, 1984 by International Bible Society. Used by permission of Zondervan. All rights reserved.

Scripture references marked KJV are from the King James Version of the Bible.

Permission notices for the lyrics that appear on each chapter title page are listed on page 219, which hereby becomes a part of this copyright page.

Any Internet addresses (websites, blogs, etc.) and telephone numbers printed in this book are offered as a resource. They are not intended in any way to be or imply an endorsement by Zondervan, nor does Zondervan vouch for the content of these sites and numbers for the life of this book.

All rights reserved. No part of this publication may be reproduced, stored in a retrieval system, or transmitted in any form or by any means — electronic, mechanical, photocopy, recording, or any other — except for brief quotations in printed reviews, without the prior permission of the publisher.

Interior design by Beth Shagene

Printed in the United States of America

09 10 11 12 13 14 • 23 22 21 20 19 18 17 16 15 14 13 12 11 10 9 8 7 6 5 4 3 2 1

To my son, John Michael—

I pray that you run faster, reach higher,
and dream bigger than I ever do.
But most of all, I pray that
you honor God in everything you do
and that my life will be an example
and give you a track to run on.

Until the Whole World Hears,
Dad

CONTENTS

FOREWORD

My wife's mother was also her sixth-grade math teacher. Thirty or so kids had Mrs. Preston as a teacher. But Denalyn had Mrs. Preston as a mother and a teacher.

When Denalyn told me this, I asked her, "What did you call her—'Mom' or 'Mrs. Preston'?"

She said, "I called her 'Mrs. Preston,' but with a different tone."

Some people speak of Jesus with a different tone—a special affection, a personal tenderness. He is a teacher—but he's also one of the family. He instructs, but also nourishes, feeds, and tucks you in at night. He isn't just "Jesus"—he's *your* Jesus.

Don't you want to know your Jesus? Of course you do. That's why you're holding this book. That's why I'm recommending it. Mark Hall doesn't have any secrets or undiscovered formulas. But he does have great insights and a wonderful way of sharing them.

Who knows? By the end of the book you may realize that Jesus is not just a teacher at the front of the class, but the One who takes you home at the end of the day.

MAX LUCADO

WHY WE NEED OUR OWN JESUS

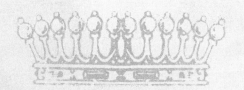

THIS MORNING, I AWOKE EXHAUSTED FROM THE weirdest dream. I was slogging through a battlefield, fighting some unidentified enemy in a war without explanation.

So I was already drained when I realized I couldn't eat breakfast because some buddies and I were starting a fast today. It seemed like such a good idea a few days ago. All of this was bouncing around in my head as I got into my new car only to remember it doesn't have AM radio. I'm trying to wean myself off talk radio because it tells me a thousand times over that the world is going to pot. *Great. Another fast on an already difficult morning.*

Then I reached my office at Eagle's Landing First Baptist Church and encountered a secretary who wasn't wearing her customary smile. She pointed at her watch and told me I was late in placing my first phone call for a series of scheduled media interviews. That only reminded me I needed some time to work on new songs for the next album. Then there's the upcoming tour ...

If a barometer could measure the degree of being flustered, my needle would have been nearing the red side.

Yet at some point during the first interview I started thinking, *Man, God is good. Shut up and deal with this. This is awesome.* I started talking about everything God is doing with Casting Crowns and with our ministry at church, and I got pumped. Later, I ran into someone who asked, "Hey, what do you think about your record being number two in the Billboard 200?" All I could say was, "That's pretty awesome," but inside I was doing cartwheels and praising the Lord. My tense morning was a distant memory. Life was good.

Then came the email.

I learned of a problem with one of the kids in our student ministry, and my heart sank. Right about then, someone showed up for another big appointment I had forgotten about, and a crammed day lost another hour. I found myself feeling gravity again.

So I've been up and down from the moment I awoke. All of this happened today. And it's only 11:00 a.m.

I sure am glad I have my own Jesus. If I didn't have my own personal walk with him, my life would be one giant vat of emotion, a tempest tossing me from one whim to the next. Which is why I have learned *I need my own Jesus*—my own relationship with the Lord of all creation. I can't live by what I feel but by the truth God's Word reveals.

This last line may sound familiar because it's part of the bridge in "East to West"—a song I wrote about learning to accept and live in the reality of God's forgiveness. The lyrics describe where I've been in my walk with Jesus over the past few years. No matter how many times my old life comes haunting, God calls me to rest on his truth and not on what I feel or think.

As Christians, we can't live by what we feel or go off our gut, because it is rotten (Philippians 3:19). We have to live by truth. God has been constantly reminding me lately that his Word is truth. And truth is truth. It doesn't only become truth when we start believing it. Truth just *is*—for everybody everywhere and at all times.

I try to rest in that fact and not in how I feel about it or what it means to me. Who cares what the Bible means *to me*? We need to know what it *means*. That's where I have to allow God to redefine my thinking. He tells us in Romans 12:2 not to be conformed to this world but to be transformed by the renewal of our minds. What always gets me about this verse is he's telling believers we still need to be transformed. It means I have a saved spirit but I still think with a lost brain, and slowly but surely my mind has to be transformed. Such transformation comes but one way — by truth. By his Word.

Knowing What You Believe

Back in 1998, one of my former students called me a few months into his freshman year in college. He attended an institution of higher learning, yet he wanted answers to a kind of test he didn't expect.

"Man, I need help," he said, his voice almost a quiver. "These professors are pounding me. The entire culture here is mocking everything I ever heard you say."

He spent the next several minutes asking questions, though one unsettled me more than any of the others. He told the story of an assertion someone made in class that left him too befuddled to reply, which is why he had called me for help.

"Now, what do I believe about that again?" he asked.

Less than a year after leaving the cozy spiritual nest of our church group, where everyone shared the same beliefs and lingo, he was facing the white-hot furnace of a hostile universe and its ungodly worldviews. And he folded like paper in fire.

He didn't have his own Jesus.

I'm not saying he hadn't experienced salvation; he simply didn't have a meaningful connection to a living Lord through his own intimate fellowship. The walk, what little existed, wasn't personal. Reading between his worry lines, I could hear his confession: "Mark, I don't really have my own beliefs. I just have yours, and you're not here. I don't know how I'm going to get through this. Your Jesus didn't come to college with me."

At first, I wondered whether this young man needed some instruction in apologetics to inform his answers in an ungodly environment. The more he talked, and the more I thought about it, I concluded he needed something else, something deeper than quick answers from a book or enrollment in a discipleship course. He needed his own Jesus, his own nurtured, daily fellowship with the one true God. He wasn't cultivating his own faith, much less living off of it.

Learning a Few Lessons

Recently, I've been learning some hard lessons. First, I can't forge spiritual transformation or growth. I'm not the Holy Spirit. I can teach biblical truths and try to reach people through song, but I can't make someone listen or even care—let alone change. My responsibility is to tell the truth in love as God grants the opportunity.

Second, many of us believers, even longtime members of the body of Christ, have genuine *faith* but parasitic *practices*. Sometimes our only experiences with God have trickled down secondhand from the lives of more mature believers. What we know of an authentic walk with God actually belongs to someone else—it isn't grounded in our own experience of God.

This book was generated as I asked myself—as I now ask you—some difficult questions. Is your walk with Jesus Christ characterized by personal faith, personal prayer, personal study, and personal disciplines? Or do you get by with the overflow from more mature Christians?

Do you have your own Jesus?

Perhaps reading these words makes you uncomfortable. The notion sounds almost heretical.

Your own Jesus.

Yet the longer I walk with and serve Jesus in the local church, the more crucial the question seems. Every believer must have his or her own Jesus, for Jesus is the only way to salvation, peace, and contentment, both in this world and the next.

It sounds weird. It sounds like I'm insisting you find your own way, as though there are as many versions of Jesus out there as there are people. In fact, there is only one — and he is the only true way (John 14:6), and he is the same yesterday and today and forever (Hebrews 13:8). What has multiplied is the number of fragmented, faulty, *human-generated* Jesus versions.

This is precisely why you must have your own Jesus — your own personal walk with the one true Jesus.

Everything in life stems from our walk with God. We need our own, everyday, walking-around friendship with God. Just him. I'm using "your own Jesus" to convey just how much God insists on the personal.

Your pastor can pour into you. Your small group leader can pour into you. Your favorite band can pour into you. All of these folks are terrific, and they'll encourage you in your walk with Jesus — but you will have nothing more than empty religion until you develop your own friendship with the Lord. You can learn from others, but they can't live your life for you.

You must pursue Christ for yourself. You must find your own Jesus.

The Jesus.

Finding the Rhythm of God's Heartbeat

The apostle Paul writes in his letter to the Ephesians, "There is one body and one Spirit—just as you were called to the one hope that belongs to your call—one Lord, one faith, one baptism, one God and Father of all, who is over all and through all and in all" (4:4–6).

If we stop reading there, however, we miss a key component. The next verse clues us into the truth that Jesus, the "one God" to whom Paul refers, must be ours in a personal way: "But grace was given to *each one of us* according to the measure of Christ's gift" (Ephesians 4:7, emphasis mine). The passage's context speaks to the uniqueness of each believer as God apportions spiritual gifts for the benefit of the church. God made you unique because he wants a fellowship that is uniquely for the two of you—Jesus and you.

But how do we maintain a fellowship with God that makes us his voice, his arms and feet and hands?

The question contains the answer. Fellowship. Communion with God. The personal disciplines of Bible study, prayer, obedience, and practicing the presence of the Holy Spirit. There are no shortcuts.

Yet this book is about more than reinforcing essential spiritual disciplines. I want us to avoid something that will short-circuit our time with God. I want to help us learn to recognize and overcome the seemingly incessant opportunities for compromise, great and small, that neutralize so many believers.

Compromise is the assassin of fellowship with God. We'll learn how to spot potential compromise and, through growth in the Lord, wade through the muck and emerge resembling Jesus rather than feeling so guilty and hopeless.

All of it is designed to inspire us to find the rhythm of God's heartbeat, to obey God's bidding even in the simplest of matters, and to submit to a Lord who died for us and asks us to live for him. I can think of no more important subject for the church today, because *as go the individual walks of believers, so goes the body of Christ.*

I'm so passionate about this subject that I urge you to visit *www.castingcrowns.com,* select "Blogs," and click on "Mark Hall's Blog." Take some time in the coming days to supplement your reading of this book with a series of videos titled "Crowns' Camp." They touch on many of this book's themes.

And as we're told in John 15:5, Jesus is the vine, and

we are the branches. He grafted us in, each branch a unique part of the growing vine. It has to be individual. It has to be real. It has to be personally cultivated. You have to be able to call Jesus your own.

CHAPTER 1

EXPLAINING THE WIND

East to West

I can't live by what I feel
But by the truth your Word reveals
I'm not holding on to you
But you're holding on to me

THE GUN FELT AS COLD AS DECEMBER IN MY hand. I could see my friend ordering a cone in the yogurt store while I sat alone in his car with a lonely heart, my dark thoughts, and his gun.

She had dumped me. The holiday season in my hometown of Montgomery, Alabama, thickened my misery. My girlfriend enjoyed the ring my nineteen-year-old heart had given her for Christmas and celebrated by dumping me. (In her defense, she is now a wonderful Christian woman and godly mother.) To this day, I have never felt lower than I did during that holly, jolly Christmas.

I stared at my buddy in the store but really didn't

see him. I thought about the girl. And then I thought about the gun.

Scarred Hands

I had accepted Jesus into my heart ten years earlier at Eastdale Baptist Church's Vacation Bible School (VBS). That summer, a caravan of trucks paraded through my neighborhood while kids handed out candy and balloons, yelling, "Come to Vacation Bible School! Come to Vacation Bible School!"

Since the kids looked like they'd come from a fun factory, I talked my parents into letting me go. When VBS ended, this church did something more churches need to do—they followed up. Someone came to my house and thanked my parents for taking me to VBS. Mom and Dad visited the church the following Sunday.

The death of Jeff Money, a buddy I played with when I visited my grandparents' home, further softened my parents' hearts. When he drowned in the city swimming pool, it rocked my family. My parents' eyes were opened when they saw the Money family demonstrate incredible faith in Jesus after their boy's death.

James Blakeney, Eastdale's minister of music, led my thirty-three-year-old dad to the Lord, and Dad jumped into faith with abandon. Attending church became the glue to our week. Dad did construction work for the church and helped people move furniture. He joined the choir, even though he'd never really sung before. He grew as a vocalist and invited his nervous son onstage with him—he's the reason I'm a singer today.

As a nine-year-old, I listened to Pastor Wayne Burns preach about my need to be forgiven of my sins. His words cut straight to my heart. I saw other people go forward to pray and get baptized. It was all laid out in front of me, and I thought on it. Then one Sunday morning, I realized, "I need this. I need Jesus in my heart." I asked Jesus to forgive me of my sins and take over my life.

At that moment, Jesus, my own Savior, removed my sins from me as far as the east is from the west (Psalm 103:12)—from one scarred hand to the other.

The Dumbest Thought

A decade later, I still didn't grasp the truth that my sin had been erased. I just knew the same heart that had Jesus in it still hurt like never before. I had spent two years in a dating relationship building my life around a girl. I learned what happens when you build your life around a person and then the person leaves: you don't have a life anymore.

In that yogurt store parking lot, I thought about ending it all. I didn't think I had much of a life to end. I'd considered suicide before, but when my buddy showed off his pistol, something happened inside of me. When he left me alone in his car, death became a real possibility. I didn't understand it then, but spiritual warfare had descended.

Satan hissed at me. Do it. *Do it.* He clenched his teeth and urged me on. *Get it over with.*

I sat there holding the gun, listening to that still wrong voice. My fingers curled around the cold metal grip.

And then I had the dumbest thought.

The dumbest thought that opened my heart to understanding forgiveness. The dumbest thought that propelled me into ministry, marriage to the girl of my dreams, and a music career.

The dumbest thought that saved my life.

The White Monster

Growing up, I loved horror movies. I begged my parents to let me stay up and watch scary movies into the wee hours. At the time, Hollywood offered movies like *Alien* and *Friday the 13th*, but my parents didn't let me know those even existed. To me, a horror movie meant a black-and-white Frankenstein flick or Bela Lugosi playing Dracula.

During commercial breaks in those late-night monster fests, Dad would dispatch me on suddenly urgent errands. He would concoct a strange need, something intended to test me—and amuse him.

"Son," he'd begin seriously, his face illuminated by the flickering television set in our darkened family room, "go to the storage shed in the backyard and get me a screwdriver."

I arched one eyebrow. "What? It's midnight!"

Dad just looked at me, so out I trudged to the toolshed behind our home. The southern Alabama night enfolded our yard like a vampire's cloak, and my feet felt cold in the dew-soaked grass. I tried not to let my imagination run wild, but I was secretly glad that at least I'd have a screwdriver for a weapon on the trip back to the house.

As I fumbled around with twitchy fingers to find the screwdriver, the hairs on the back of my neck began to stand at attention. Did I mention our shed didn't have a light?

On my way back to the house, my dogs went ballistic. I *knew* they weren't barking at me. One second, my loving little wiener dogs were nipping at my feet, and the next they went Cujo on some unseen danger. I almost needed fresh pajamas.

Just before I panicked, my dad appeared at the back door and flipped on the porch light. There, just a few yards ahead of me, I caught a glimpse of a menacing white creature with a long tail as it hissed at my little dachshunds. My parents hadn't let me see *Halloween*, but somehow I could hear the theme music playing.

To fathom my confusion in the ensuing seconds, you have to understand I had never laid eyes on a live possum. I had seen dead possums decaying along the highway, but breezing past roadkill at fifty-five miles per hour doesn't do the little boogers justice.

They're stone-cold killers, man.

When you don't understand something new, your brain compensates — otherwise, it would just explode on the spot and ooze out your ears. For instance, if you'd never seen a horse before, you might say, "That's the biggest dog I've ever seen."

At that terrible midnight moment in the backyard, I knew I was looking at the world's biggest rat. Enormously big. It-might-eat-me-in-one-bite big.

The possum was albino. He had white fur and pink-rimmed bluish eyes that reflected the porch light. His lips were so pink they looked almost red. I tried to stay calm, but then I saw its teeth. They were enormous. They looked like rows of white needles. I can still see the beast in my mind, crouched, back arched, teeth ready to rend. Every late-night scary movie I'd ever seen was condensed into a single hellish furball.

What happened next came close to scarring me for life. Dad hustled over, grabbed a shovel from the shed, and ... bong! He knocked the possum cold and proceeded to chop it to bits right in front of me. Then he calmly put the shovel back in the shed, walked past me without a word, and went inside to watch the rest of the movie.

I didn't need horror movies — Dr. Frankenstein lived just down the hall.

My chest heaved as I scurried back to the living room. I folded my hands in my lap and stared at the television. The monsters on the screen seemed like kid's play compared to what I had just witnessed.

Dad peeked over at me and smiled. He explained that he had just killed a possum — something that was more of a pest than a threat. His calming words went in one ear and out the other. My rapid-fire heartbeat convinced me that I had just seen a monster, no matter what Dad told me.

Flawed Logic

It took a while to process the possum sighting, but years later, I realized I had had a typical reaction. My brain operated like anyone else's when confronted by something new and shocking: logic kicked in.

We take the same approach with the Bible, and especially with forgiveness. We hold forgiveness up to the light, inspect it from every conceivable angle, shake it, thump it, and bring it to our ear to see if it's ever going to say something back to us. Then we decide it's too good to be true. We let our logic elbow faith out of the way.

After all, God-sized forgiveness doesn't compute. It just makes sense that God will give up on us sooner or later.

Understanding and truly accepting God's forgiveness is the incubator to a meaningful walk with Jesus. As we escape the dregs of compromise to walk in purity and obedience, we are free to grow on God's timetable if we ignore the lies of the unholy world. And only by avoiding faulty human logic can we give our lives over to the seeming risk of a God who is actually unable to be anything but faithful.

Everything we will ever be or ever have in our walks with our own Jesus hinges on this simple truth. It is a truth comprised of one word and yet all of eternity.

F-A-I-T-H.

You'll have to take God at his word before your outlook and your walk breathe life. The New Testament Greek for the word *believe* is *pisteuo*—as in John 3:16: "For God so loved the world, that he gave his only Son, that whoever *pisteuo*s in him should not perish but have eternal life." The word *pisteuo* means "trust" and carries with it the connotation of placing all of your weight on something.

When you sat down to read this book, you *pisteuo*ed probably either in a chair or a bed. You trusted in it to bear your weight, hold you up, and not drop you.

Do you have *pisteuo* faith, the kind in which you place all of your weight on Jesus for now and eternity? It is the only faith able to open the doors of heaven and unlock your eternal destiny. But it requires leaning on Jesus and carrying on a daily fellowship with him that can't help but uplift him and change you. It has to be personal. God insists on it.

I say this with confidence because we can't mature in Christ until we understand we are positioned *in* Christ. Read the letter to the Ephesians and notice how many times it asserts that our position is in Christ. This truth deepens our understanding of Romans 8:1: "There is therefore now no condemnation for those who are *in* Christ Jesus" (emphasis added).

We can either believe what our Father tells us and grow or listen to the Lie and die. The Lie comes from Satan, who burdens us with guilt and shame. But let's start fresh. Let's ditch the Lie and believe the assurances of our loving Father.

The Bible says we are forgiven. It says we are saints. It says we are children of God, citizens of heaven, members of God's family, and chosen members of a royal priesthood. It says we are salt and light, we are people who dwell in a city set on a hill. It says we are co-heirs with Christ, ready to inherit the eternal life reserved for the saints. We cannot be separated from the love of God that is in Christ Jesus.

As believers, sometimes we feel such basic truths are below us. Shouldn't we be discoursing on God's sovereignty or immutability or debating predestination and our millennial views? Forgiveness and trust are for beginners — they're for the VBS kids handing out candy from the back of a truck.

Yet when your world is crashing around you, what are you really wrestling with? In tough times you ask, "Can I really trust God with this situation? Am I being punished for all the bad stuff I've done? Is God really going to forgive me? Is my sin really gone?"

Logic says one thing, but God says another.

Inexplicable Favor

God's forgiveness is without precedence. When I forgive someone, what that person did to me seems always to hover in the back of my mind. I can't help but make decisions based on my memory of what happened. How can God, whose memory is perfect, be any different? We assume there's no way God can forgive without condition and without end.

But that's human logic. If we're uncertain about what God says in his Word, we'll think, "I'm not really sure what God's love is, but this is what my dad's love is like, so that must be what God's love is like." Or, "Since forgiveness looks like this at work or at school, this must be how God forgives."

Sometimes that logic is fine—you can live the rest of your life thinking that possums are rats—but mistaken notions about forgiveness can shatter lives.

We live as if we believe that God follows human logic. Three strikes, and you're out. You get written up so many times, and you're fired. You get so many reprimands, and you're suspended. You get too many speeding tickets, and you lose your license. You break these vows, and your spouse leaves you.

You commit this sin too many times, and God is going to leave you too. It just makes sense.

This logic originates with our false belief that we did something to make God love us in the first place. We think we're so lovable that God can't help but love us. But really the opposite is true. While we were still sinners, Christ died for us. God cared for us before we were even born!

When we understand that our relationship with God is something he starts, maintains, and completes (Philippians 1:6), we can begin to accept the truth that God's forgiveness is forever. As Psalm 103:11–12 assure us,

> For as high as the heavens are above the
>   earth,
>   so great is his steadfast love toward those
>   who fear him;
> as far as the east is from the west,
>   so far does he remove our transgressions
>   from us.

During my junior year of high school, Mr. Short taught my church small group. I liked him because he was different. He wasn't the polished, tie-wearing, churchy, old-school guy I had come to expect. He was raw in his approach, more direct. He would hit us with statements and make us think. His class was the Baptist version of *Dead Poets Society*. Mr. Short wouldn't allow us to give Sunday school answers but tried to cut through our little churchy shells. He refused to let us fake it. He wanted us to know why we believed what we believed.

One day, Mr. Short explained God's forgiveness by using Psalm 103 in a way I will always remember: "There is a reason God used the east and west to describe how far he cast your sin from you," he said. "If you go north, you can only go north so far until you're finally going south. And you can only go south so far until you're going north. But if you start traveling east, it keeps going east forever, and west just keeps going west. If you think about it, you're never going to go so far west that you're going east. That's how far he cast our sin from us."

It Is Finished

God says he drops our sins into his sea of forgetfulness (Isaiah 43:25; Micah 7:19). Sometimes we believers struggle on that sea, riding its swells and billows to the point of sickness as we base our worth and identity on worldly pursuits and opinions. No one else forgets our sin. A sea of forgetfulness doesn't make sense when everyone else is ready to throw us into a mud puddle of remembrance. The world continually reminds us of our failure and rubs our noses in it.

The most liberating truth in all of Scripture is that *we are liberated.* God is not a God bound by human logic. God is not like our spouse or coworker. God is not like our teacher, friend, or significant other. When God says he forgives us, he is speaking the truth because *he* is truth (1 Thessalonians 2:13; Titus 1:2). When God says he forgives, he isn't talking about a sappy, sentimental moment in which we talked him into being good to us. He is referring to a sovereign decree of his will to extend grace to an undeserving person.

He did this by killing his Son.

This is a blunt statement, but it's true. John 3:16 states that God *gave* his Son. At the same time, Jesus, who is God, laid down his life (John 10:17 – 18). Why? So he could offer us the truth of 2 Corinthians 5:21: "For He made Him who knew no sin to be sin for us, that we might become the righteousness of God in Him" (NKJV).

Jesus became sin for us. Gnaw on that one. That's how serious God is about forgiveness.

With no equivocation, God says, "I am choosing not

to count your sin against you anymore—not because you're a good person or because you're doing more good than bad—but because my Son paid the debt for your sin. *Tetelestai*—it is finished (John 19:30). Transaction complete. All you have to do is believe me and give me your whole life, and I'll place your sin upon my Son and credit his righteousness to you.

"I'm doing every bit of this. You're doing nothing. Even the faith you demonstrate will be my gift to you. Now live as though your sin is gone—because it is. As far as the east is from the west."

Every Crevice

Every human being since Adam and Eve has sinned. Each of us is a sinner, enslaved to the sinful nature within us. This is why Jesus told Nicodemus he must be "born again" (John 3:3). Our lone hope is to be made new through spiritual rebirth in Jesus, and the only way to produce fruit afterward is to live as though we believe God did what he said he did.

We will never understand these truths fully—that's why faith is required. Even Nicodemus, steeped in the laws and traditions of Israel, struggled with the notion. Jesus smiled at him on a breezy Jerusalem night and said, "Do not marvel that I said to you, 'You must be born again.' The wind blows where it wishes, and you hear its sound, but you do not know where it comes from or where it goes. So it is with everyone who is born of the Spirit" (John 3:7–8).

It's OK not to see the wind; it's enough to know that God makes it blow.

The next time you find yourself saying, "Well, surely God will do this," or, "There's no way God would do that," ask yourself if Scripture backs you up or if you're creating theology based on human logic. God's character is revealed to us only after the Holy Spirit quickens us through his living Word. He speaks truth into every crevice of our lives and holds us accountable (Hebrews 4:13).

With unyielding and unflinching love, God insists we change our lives and draw ever closer. God invites us past the personal to the intimate. God invites us to be Christlike.

We'll never be able to explain how our sins are removed from us as far as the east is from the west. But each day we *are* able to accept God's forgiveness in faith. Accepting God's forgiveness means appreciating it and living in a way that shows we appreciate it. It means being willing to forgive ourselves (John 4; 8:1–12) and to forgive others (Matthew 6:14–15).

Having my sin removed as a nine-year-old was one thing; allowing that truth to change my life was another. That wouldn't happen until a decade later, when I decided to let the Word of God—and not a bullet—pierce my mind.

Cleanup Is Always Messy

My friend Ronnie stood in the yogurt shop as I sat in his car and held his gun. As I listened to the urgent lies of Satan—*Do it! End it!*—the dumbest thought saved me: *"I don't want to mess up my friend's car."*

That was my reason for living.

I didn't want my buddy to have to drive a car in which I had splattered my blood and brains. I refused to do that to him. I put down the gun and threw my hands into the air. "God, obviously I'm not going about this relationship thing the right way."

It was a watershed moment. Until then, a "relationship" with God meant going to church. It never occurred to me I needed more depth. I saw adults who were serious about their faith, but I never saw anybody my age with a sincere walk. Since I seemed to be normal, I figured I was on-track spiritually.

My breakup and my near suicide changed me. I

thought, "Maybe there's more to this. God, I need to give you more of my life."

I still didn't know what that meant. Despite sitting in church for more than ten years, my theology and faith were shallow. But over the next few months, three events would change the course of my life: I sensed a tug toward ministry; I began dating my future wife, Melanie; and I started singing songs in my head for the first time.

Several months later, at Baptist College of Florida in Graceville, I met a friend named Bill Jessup and discovered someone my age who was abandoned to Jesus. In my spiritual dullness, the way he lived seemed crazy.

Bill talked about God all the time. He wasn't weird or preachy, but he'd say things like, "Man, I'm really praying about this thing that's going on in my life." Or he'd say, "Pray for Cindy and me. We're worried about finances this week, and we'll be praying for you." Or he'd say, "Hey, check out this verse. It really meant a lot to me in my quiet time this morning."

I thought, "This is insane. This is so foreign to me." The truth took a while to soak in: This walk-with-God thing is an everyday friendship; it's not just a Sunday morning add-on.

The slow dawn grew brighter. The Lord wanted all of me.

Tearing Down the Walls

It's no wonder it was hard to hear the voice of Jesus above the lies of Satan. Just like the rich young ruler, I had slotted my life into isolated compartments. School occupied one space. Church fit over here, music over there, and movies next to that. Parents here and friends there. All nice and tidy—and most of them closed off from Jesus.

Until one day Bill and another friend, Jon Dorsey, yanked all my compartmentalized drawers out onto the floor.

I stared and realized I was an utter mess.

One moment I sang in church; the next I rocked out to profane music in my car. One moment I shared in Bible study class; the next I rented another R-rated horror movie I so enjoyed. Bill and Jon spoke truth to me, and I had to own up to it.

The battle raged throughout the year I spent in my first ministry job as youth pastor at New Zion Baptist Church in Bethlehem, Florida. Then the struggle followed me to First Baptist Church in Samson, Alabama. The sins I tried to lay down kept rising back up. I grew quieter about my choices around friends like Bill and Jon. My favorite pursuits and ways of thinking conflicted with what they said and how they lived. Yet I knew they spoke truth. They kept opening this really powerful book and pointing to verses.

Then came the guilt.

"Here I am saying to students that I'm all of these lofty things and spitting out Scripture at everybody," I muttered. "Here I am saying I'm going to be a minister who leads people and sings in front of crowds, and yet I'm not practicing what I preach."

I can see how some might joke, "Wow, R-rated movies. He really took a dark and twisted path." But as I dug deeper into God's Word, I discovered verses such as James 1:13 – 15, which I'll unpack in detail in the next chapter. It tells us that sin is "conceived" from within us. It starts in our hearts and minds. This truth convicted me. I wanted to be holy, just as God is holy (1 Peter 1:15 – 16).

Any darkness that comes out in my life is the fruit of my own appetites, and it's my choice either to feed or starve those appetites. I was purposely feeding on music and movies with dark, violent themes and plenty of sexual content. All of that takes root in our thought lives and affects everything we do. It clouds our communication with God and can limit how he uses us. If someone is in a dark place and needs help, we're probably not going to have suitable answers when we're gorging on trash.

I felt I was at a crossroads.

I remember the crisp air one night before a church service in Samson. Cars drove past on Main Street, illuminating the brick walls with moving light. I was going to be singing in ten minutes, and I was sick of myself.

"Lord, you don't have my life, do you? You just have pieces of me," I said. "You have sections of me, and you're inside me, but it's like I'm holding you in and keeping you from spilling over into all of these other areas. I don't want you to get into my business."

My pasty tongue clung to the roof of my mouth and my chest thumped. I knew I needed to change.

"Father, I have to give you lordship here, and I have to lay down some things."

Part of me had to go away.

I thought, "My Father, who loves me, who walks with me, who knows me and sees things in my life that are tearing me down, is now trying to free me from them." It was a revelation. My blinders fell off, and I knew my relationship with God would follow his design instead of mine. I knew I was beginning to understand the fundamental point of forgiveness.

What shall we say then? Are we to continue in sin that grace may abound? By no means! How can we who died to sin still live in it? Do you not know that all of us who have been baptized into Christ Jesus were baptized into his death? We were buried therefore with him by baptism into death, in order that, just as Christ was raised from the dead by the glory of the Father, we too might walk in newness of life.

ROMANS 6:1–4

So I did. I walked inside the church, and as the music started, I began to sing a new song.

CHAPTER 2

INFINITE

Slow Fade

The journey from your mind to your hands
Is shorter than you're thinking
Be careful if you think you stand
You just might be sinking

Blue has a dark, bushy ponytail and tattoos on each side of a neck framed by stud earrings. A tattoo of a nail jutting from his flesh adorns the inside of each wrist. His friends gave him the nickname, and it stuck. It was either that or Paluku, the tag given to firstborn boys like him in Zaire, Africa, where his parents served as missionaries. Blue is the oldest of four children, and the only son.

Maybe that explains his protective instincts when mortars began exploding outside of his house in Zaire. Lying on the floor, twelve-year-old Paluku white-knuckled a curved machete, his only defense against the murdering, raping mob going door-to-door. *Paluku.* Firstborn son.

First to die.

In 1992, Blue anticipated his first Christmas in Africa. He'd been a preacher's kid, and now he was a missionary kid too. Was he to become a statistic as well?

The town of Goma, Zaire, perched on the northeast shore of massive Lake Kivu, was the occasional target for a marauding military. "Apparently the Zairean military was underpaid," Blue said. "So the government would let them go out and loot the town as kind of a reimbursement."

That evening, Blue was playing in his front yard when he heard the first pistol rounds. Rifle shots followed, then the automatic fire of AK−47s. Like a hard drinker warming to his task, the military soon reached for the hard stuff. Blue's dad waved him inside long before the mortars strobed the skyline.

At the entrance to Blue's street, the military started going house-to-house. The gunshots grew louder, the mortar explosions closer, the screaming voices more familiar. Blue's dad, Shayne, crouched the family between the brick walls of the hallway. Blue couldn't tell if the vibrations came from the thick walls shaking or from his pounding heart.

Shayne darted to the bathroom, grabbing a framed copy of Psalm 91 from the wall. Blue had used the bathroom every day without bothering to read the psalm. Shayne improvised as he prayed it over his family. *"You will not fear the terror of the night, nor the bullet that flies by day."* Then he grabbed a machete and moved his adolescent son with him closer to the front door.

"I don't know all that went on in each house. It was typical for them to rape the women and to occasionally kill the people—but definitely to rob," Blue said. "My father and I were lying on the floor on either side of the hall doorway, staring through the living room at the front door about fifteen feet away. It was glass and had bars on it. All the windows had bars. We weren't allowed to have guns, so we had two *pangas*, curved machetes. My dad gave me the machete and said, 'When they come in, let them take whatever they want. If they want the TV, if they want your keyboard, whatever it is, let them take it. But if they try to touch your mom or your sisters, I want you to know that you're going to die. But I want you to kill as many of them as you can before you die to give your mother and sisters a better chance.' I remember looking out of the hallway, holding on to this machete and staring at the door, waiting for these men to walk up."

The screams and gunshots grew louder, closer. So did Psalm 91:

> For he will command his angels concerning
>> you
>> to guard you in all your ways.
> On their hands they will bear you up,
>> lest you strike your foot against a stone.
>>>> PSALM 91:11–12

Suddenly it was silent.

"It never came. It never came," Blue said twice, as if still trying to convince himself, staring as he replayed the scene in his mind. "We heard it as they got to the outside of the gate, but then everything just went silent for a minute. I was twelve years old, but that was the longest silence I've ever heard. And then it just passed. The noise picked back up and continued down the street past us, but we didn't know what happened. We were sitting there reading this psalm, so we associated it with that."

The next day, Blue's family crossed over the nearby border to Ginsenyi, Rwanda, to stay for two weeks until the chaos subsided. When they returned home, a woman selling vegetables approached Blue's mother.

"Do you know why the soldiers didn't hit your house

that night?" she asked. The question caught Blue's mom off guard.

"That night I was on the street," she said, "and they grabbed me and said, 'Point out to us who has money.'"

Blue's family's shipping containers still hadn't arrived from the United States, so they had little. They rode everywhere on bicycles. "They're Americans," the woman told the soldiers. "But they don't have money."

It didn't stop the soldiers. Consumed with the idea of looting Americans, they headed toward the missionaries' gate. Suddenly they stopped and stared, their guns falling silent.

"These are military soldiers, fully armed," Blue said. "As they approached our gate, they said they saw tall men standing around our house, and it scared them. They refused to go in. They progressed to the next street."

"For he will command his angels concerning you to guard you in all your ways."

Fading Slowly

My life verse is really a life chapter—Psalm 1. The chapter is succinct but says everything I need for godly living.

Blessed is the man
    who walks not in the counsel of the wicked,
nor stands in the way of sinners,
    nor sits in the seat of scoffers;
but his delight is in the law of the Lord,
    and on his law he meditates day and night.

Psalm 1:1–2

For years, I concentrated on one segment: "But his delight is in the law of the Lord, and on his law he meditates day and night." I've always struggled with discipline and guarding my time with the Lord, so that verse hit a nerve. Then one day I took the passage's advice and meditated on it. The scales fell off. I saw something new.

I saw the slow fade of a person.

Psalm 1 reveals that we have the potential to go from delighting in God's Word to walking with the wicked, standing with sinners, and, ultimately, sitting in the seat of scoffers. This descent is what happens to the person who does not delight in God's Word. Every authentic believer has a genuine desire for the Word of God and delights in it. If that hunger is not there, something is amiss.

Let's begin at the beginning: Our counsel is what initiates a slow fade. Our counsel comes from several outlets. The people we hang around with. The places we go. The music, movies, and television we consume. The websites we click on, and the jokes we laugh at.

Psalm 1 lays out Satan's plan of attack. He'll go after our counsel and try to influence us with the logic and worldly wisdom of others. If Satan can trip us into thinking more and more like the world thinks, he has greased the skids for a slow fade.

Whatever the person in Psalm 1 pours in will eventually spill out. That's how he or she goes from delighting to sitting.

Once we heed improper counsel, we are standing in the way of sinners. Life is different now. We say we believe this God stuff, but the world doesn't think we look much different. We're standing right there with them in the way of sinners, even though we claim the narrow way of Jesus.

If this is true, the world figures, then Jesus must not be who he claimed to be either.

Any Christian can fall. I've seen families that everyone admires crumble. I've seen teenagers with a love for God and a passion for reaching people give it all away for a little more popularity. I've seen pastors fail their flocks.

It's not uncommon to find yourself in church one day, zoned-out and thinking, "What in the world happened to me? Why am I so numb and incapable of caring? I know I'm far away, but why don't I want to get closer? How did I get here?"

It's not as if you enjoy an awesome you-and-God time, go to bed, wake up in the morning, and — bam! — crash and burn. It never happens that way. It's a slow process, a series of compromises by which you descend from delighting in God to sitting with the scoffers and mocking your former faith.

Our counsel is our foundation. Who and what am I allowing to influence me? Am I delighting in the Lord? Am I sowing to the Spirit, or am I sowing to the flesh? (See Galatians 6:8.)

Remember that you're not the first person Satan has ever messed with. He went to war against God, so launching an attack on you isn't going to give him any pause. He finds out where your buttons are and starts punching. One little compromise leads to another until you find yourself at a place you never thought you'd be, doing things you never thought you'd do.

But because it happens so slowly, so incrementally, you have time to rationalize every small sin along the way.

Wise Counsel

To delight in the law of the Lord is to absorb infinitely wise counsel. The believer has no greater need. Such counsel teaches us God's perfect Word and reveals to us the character and person of his Son, Jesus — and is one of the primary ways we can begin to know him for ourselves.

Our counsel consists of the people, things, and ideas that pour into us, shaping our thoughts and sparking our actions. Visit any person in jail and ask, "How did you get here?" — you'll be amazed at the number of people who reply, "Well, me and a friend were out one night ..." I don't think God is demanding that we ditch all of our friends to follow him. But if we're going to honor God with our lives, then we have to be careful about who is counseling us.

This may mean we need to limit our involvement with certain people. There are some folks we need to tell, "Hey, I love you. Let's go to lunch sometime. But you and I getting together on Friday night doesn't work for either of us." When friends have similar weaknesses or wrong motives, they can cause each other to stumble.

One biblical example comes in 2 Samuel 13, where

Amnon lusts after Tamar, his half sister. They are King David's children, born to different mothers. Amnon is so smitten with Tamar that he loses weight because he stops eating. Then comes verse 3: "But Amnon had a friend ..." Right there lies his downfall — described in that one line in the story. His friend Jonadab says, "Hey, I'll tell you what you need to do. You need to act like you're sick, and convince your dad to tell your sister to come to your bedroom to tend to you and feed you." Amnon likes the crafty ruse, does what he's told, rapes Tamar, destroys her life, and then winds up having it all come back on him through devastating consequences that follow his decisions.

The Bible is full of more subtle examples of the bad influences of others. Think about the first family: Adam fell with a little help from Eve (Genesis 3:6). Jesus' disciples constantly needled each other about who would be greatest among them (Luke 9:46–48; 22:24–27). James and John dragged their mother into the fray (Matthew 20:20–22). Jesus healed ten men with leprosy, yet only one returned to thank him; the other nine did the peer pressure thing (Luke 17:11–19).

We are who our friends are (1 Corinthians 15:33). Our friends mold our thoughts, tastes, and even our patterns of speech. What we put into our heads and hearts today will influence our choices tomorrow.

We don't prearrange life-changing moments. We don't punch a date in our cell phones to schedule our next fork in the road — they just happen. And when they do, who do we turn to? It's usually the people right beside us. We have to surround ourselves with people who stretch and challenge us, people we respect and admire and want to emulate. We hang with them and ask questions. We watch and listen more than we talk. We take wise counsel.

The Philippians Filter

What kind of counsel does our entertainment give us?

Philippians 4:8 says we're supposed to focus on things that are pure, lovely, true, noble, and just. Things that are praiseworthy and virtuous. We need to apply the Philippians filter to our lives and ask some serious questions.

Don't ask, "Is this wrong? Is this good? Is this bad?" These are questions of immaturity. It's as if we want to ask God these questions so he can show us where the line is. By doing so, we can set up our tents right there on the side of the cliff. *How close to sin can I get and still not sin?* We'd never voice that, but it's usually in our hearts.

We need to graduate from that kind of thinking. Instead, our hearts should say, "OK, if I want to honor God with my life and be an example for other people, then what's the wisest and best thing for me to put into my head?"

We should never approach entertainment by saying, "Find me a verse." "I don't see anything wrong with it." "Surely God wouldn't mind." It's the most natural thing to engage in such logical arguments, and we can talk ourselves into or out of almost anything.

What we need to ask is, "God, will this help me live the new life, or will it drag me back toward my old life?"

When I'm eating at Applebee's and an old song plays over the loudspeaker, I can tell you where I was and what I was doing when I first heard that song way back when. It's almost impossible to forget, and it's only a song. Some folks who compromise on music choices claim they listen for the music and not the lyrics. Problem is, an ever-growing little industry would disagree with the premise—an industry called advertising.

A thirty-second commercial during the 2009 Super Bowl telecast cost $3 million. It cost $2.7 million the year before. Either our viewing and listening choices affect us, or advertisers must be the dumbest people on the planet.

When we read the word *counsel* in the first verse of Psalm 1, we should notice how close it lies to another key word. The verb *walks* indicates we're going to act based on our counsel. We're either going to walk in the way of the wicked or in the way of the righteous. Our counsel points the way.

Standing Means Stopping

According to James, the half brother of Jesus, the slow fade occurs when we're entangled by our thoughts and desires. As he puts it,

> Let no one say when he is tempted, "I am being tempted by God," for God cannot be tempted with evil, and he himself tempts no one. But each person is tempted when he is lured and enticed by his own desire. Then desire when it has conceived gives birth to sin, and sin when it is fully grown brings forth death.
>
> JAMES 1:13–15

James says it all starts in my head and my heart, but the slow fade comes out in my hands and feet. If we look at our habitual struggles as the monster in the closet — always lurking — then how do we kill the monster?

Stop feeding it.

Have you ever sat in a worship service or prayer time when suddenly some nasty, improper scene from a movie that you *didn't* see pops into your head? Of course not. We planted those images inside through our own actions.

It's as though we say, "Lord, this monster is pounding me with a wooden bat. Would you please take that bat away?" The Lord helps us with that one, and then we turn around and hand the monster an aluminum bat, saying, "Try this one; it's a lot harder." We arm the beast that wants to destroy us. Bad visuals don't creep into our minds. We invite them in, hand out party favors and snacks, and get our groove on.

For a while, we can keep our tiny compromises inside, slotted nicely in the ever-deepening crevices of our minds. This is why we can appear to have it all together on the outside. The charade lasts only so long. Out of a person's heart spring the issues of life (Proverbs 4:23). Those issues will come out of our mouths and surface in our reactions to others. Just look at us believers when we are wronged by someone. When Christians are right and we know we're right, we're the most dangerous people on the planet. At least in my case, you'd better stand out of my way. I've given myself clearance to do anything I want when I'm convinced I'm right.

When we're driving and someone pulls out in front of us, man, it's like we've never made a driving mistake. *"Look at that moron!"* I always want to pull alongside and shoot out my most disgusted glance as I look down my nose and glare. There is something about that feeling of being just a little up on someone else.

Everything inside of us will come out at one time or another, even the ways in which we handle praise and success and view certain people. Sometimes well before a big sin occurs, tiny compromises affect our attitudes and opinions, leading us closer to a major fall.

First we walked in the wrong counsel. Next we decided to pause long enough to take a whiff, which left us standing with the gleeful sinners. Now we're so enmeshed in this lifestyle that we're sitting down, relaxing in a place of habitual sin with all the other scoffers. We're at a place we know we're not supposed to be, but we try not to think about it. Toys and idle pursuits fill our thoughts.

I've been there and thought, "Well, there's no way I can get back anyway. I'm too far away. God is too mad at me. He doesn't want anything to do with me." The hopelessness in such thinking feels as though it's the only reality.

When we sit down and get comfortable with our sin, we find little interest in the things of God, including worship attendance. When we do attend, we often find ourselves fighting the urge to go to the bathroom, stand in the hallway, or make a suddenly urgent phone call. We don't want to worship or dig into the sermon because we don't want to be reminded of how far we've slipped.

I've been there. My mind turned me against other people. I've been jealous of people who I knew walked with God, but somehow I convinced myself they were fakes. I've looked at someone with their hands in the air, obviously enraptured by a worshipful moment with Jesus, and thought, "They shouldn't do that. What's their problem? They just want to be seen."

Translation: "There's no way *they* can have something *I* don't have."

It hurts to think someone has a joy I don't possess. It's much easier to assume the worst of others rather than realize I might be the one with the problem.

When you're the only Christian you know with no problems, you're already sitting in the seat of a scoffer.

Dishrag

The slow fade leaves us with dirty, hardened hearts (thoughts, attitudes, motives) that will leave us with dirty, hardened hands (choices and actions).

I decided to illustrate this one day with a group of adult workers. As we prepared to lead a weekend retreat for our students, I wanted to ensure they understood the gravity of their leadership positions. I gathered them in a huge circle and asked them to close their eyes and put out their hands.

I could see the looks on their faces. Some of the ladies winced. They had no clue what to expect, but because I'm a youth pastor they knew it would be gross. I took an old dishrag, covered it in Karo syrup and dirt, and wadded it into a glob of filthy goo.

I went around the circle and placed the dishrag in each person's hands, rubbing it into their palms and all over the backs of their hands and fingers. All of them had the same reaction. They twisted their faces into the most disgusted looks. They couldn't peek, so they had no clue what the concoction was, but everyone around them heard their sighs and groans as I reached their open hands.

At the end, they all stood there, eyes shut but twitching, lips pursed. They held out their disgusting, gooey, sticky, nasty hands. I broke the tension by ratcheting it up: "Guys, let's all join hands and pray," I said.

I could hear the smacks of the hands clasping. I watched the grossed-out faces. And I knew that more than a few wanted to bolt to the nearest sink.

I started praying, and I prayed and prayed. And then I prayed some more. I prayed for everybody I could think of. I prayed for each leader by name. I prayed for the missionaries around the world. I prayed for our church, and at the end I prayed for the weekend retreat. When I said "Amen," everyone let go of each other's hands and stared at me.

"How many of you heard a single word I said?" I asked. "How many of you really felt connected to the Lord during that prayer?"

They all spoke in unison or shook their heads. "Nooooo, no, no."

I said, "Look at your hands. This is sin in your life. This is what happens when you're not walking with God and you make everything to be about yourself. The moment your hands got sticky, you didn't want anything to do with anybody in here. Everybody stopped. You didn't want to pray. Why? Because you couldn't concentrate on anything but your hands. I could tell. I could hear your sighs and knew all you wanted to do was to get the mess off your hands.

"You weren't hearing anything, you weren't saying anything, you weren't offering anything. You were totally focused on yourself. And when I asked you to join in prayer with the group, to support others and lean on others by joining hands, you didn't want anything to do with anything but meeting your own need of the moment."

The symbolic exercise seemed to hit home for many of them. I picked up an old, giant basin full of warm, soapy water and continued. "People are coming in here this weekend with their own issues, their own worries, their own drama at school and at home. They have all this stuff going on, all of these needs, and you may well end up missing all of it. If you're not where you're supposed to be in your walk with Jesus, you're not going to pick up on it, you're not going to love them, and you're not going to help them at all."

We went to prayer again. The sighs and giggles gave way to a somber hush. The adult leaders didn't care about their sticky hands anymore. They were ready to spend some time asking, "God, what is stopping my prayer life, stopping my worship, stopping my ministry, stopping me from glorifying you?"

Afterward, I took the basin and walked around the

circle again. I stopped in front of each leader. I asked them to hold out their hands as I poured the soapy water over them, washed them clean, took a towel, and dried their hands for them. Just as our loving Father does for us.

Many of these leaders are still talking about that night, because it gave a good picture of what the slow fade does. The fade turns us inward, where all we think about is ourselves, and takes us to the point of being useless for God's kingdom.

No Bottom

That dark night in Zaire offered twelve-year-old Cameron "Blue" Russell his most epic lesson in faith. What other explanation could there be for the "tall men" outside his home than as a living instance of Psalm 91? Blue witnessed God's power again during the next year after his family moved to neighboring Rwanda to get away from the madness. In Rwanda, madness didn't reign; pure evil did.

In 1994, the majority Hutus killed an estimated eight hundred thousand people, mostly minority Tutsis. On one of the genocide's first days, Blue watched through binoculars as a man on his knees begged for his life to another man riding atop an armored car. Three shots answered the man's desperate cries before the armored car crushed his dying body.

Blue's family fled Rwanda and escaped sure death when his dad raced their truck past an angry mob at a blockade. Decaying corpses littered the countryside, but the Russell family kept living off of Psalm 91:

> A thousand may fall at your side,
> ten thousand at your right hand,
> but it will not come near you.
> PSALM 91:7

Maybe Blue felt the trauma of those years in Africa; maybe he suffered a sense of detachment after leaving America and entering a strange world. Maybe his ever-present anger flared, even after asking Jesus into his heart at age five—anger unexplained and cancerous enough to prompt teenage thoughts of suicide. On one occasion, Blue found a gun and placed its barrel in his mouth but refused to pull the trigger out of fear. *How will my parents deal with it? What if I don't wake up in heaven?*

The rage would ebb and flow. Blue played his keyboard and wrote songs to dull the edges on the sharpest days. When the family returned to the States for a one-year furlough in 1996, his rage bubbled over as he tried to fit into the American culture of peer pressure and measuring up. The leaders and kids in the youth ministry at church left him feeling he didn't fit their mold. Growing more isolated, he reverted to another passion — guns.

Dirty Heart, Dirty Hands

Not long after Blue began hawking guns at Jonesboro High School just south of Atlanta, the gang members buying his wares invited him into the fold.

"It was the strangest feeling, because it was the first time I felt like I belonged," Blue said. "Which is so sad that here's the missionary kid coming back a little bit lost, and maybe if somebody would've just said, 'I can tell something's wrong. Let's figure it out,' and maybe sat me down and gave me a little bit of truth. But it was all judgment. There was no truth and love. It was truth and judgment. So the only family I felt I had were these gang members. And I was young and stupid and thought I had the world to prove, so I was willing to do anything to fit.

"It felt good because all that anger had an outlet. It was like I could let it out, and it was cool. I couldn't let it out in church because I was judged, but I could let it out there. The suicidal feelings really started to fade, because I could let out that aggression on somebody else."

He had turned sixteen. His gang buddies nicknamed him BabyBlue, spelled together and held together by the wrong brotherhood.

"When I was sixteen I came back and I found a letter I had written to myself when I was eight or nine. It read, 'To the older Cameron, I don't know what you'll be like or who you'll be, but I guess that you'll like guns and you'll like winning people to Jesus.' So there was obviously a fire there," Blue said. "I read my Bible every day growing up. I was deeply rooted in it, but I think a lot of it was religion. It was what I was taught to do. I had experienced God in a real and powerful way in Zaire, in Rwanda, and saw the power of Scripture come alive. There is no way I could deny it. I knew it. I remember at times I just felt so close to God. I remember talking to him. But one of my favorite Scriptures is in James where it says we're drawn away and enticed by our own desire, and when the desire is conceived it gives birth to sin.

"I had *a* relationship with God, but I didn't really know how to have *my* relationship with God because it was my parents' relationship with God. There wasn't a personal relationship. I remember seeing the power of

God, but then the flesh is so real," he said. "The thing with God is *seek and you will find.* The more we seek, the more he reveals himself. We have this ability to rationalize and make everything logical. No matter what we've seen in Scripture or in our lives, it means very little because we think, 'Well, it could mean this.' So we explain away the whole Bible. I think that's what happened with me. It got to the point where my flesh was so real that it became a priority. Just like the James verse says. If you're drawn away from God by that desire and you're enticed, at first you look and then you touch, and then that desire conceives into full sin and sin ultimately becomes death. In my life, that's what it was. I started giving in to the flesh a little bit earlier. I knew *of* God. In my heart I thought I loved God, but I really didn't."

A return to Africa, this time to Kenya, removed Blue from gang life. But Blue's rebellion only escalated. He refused all lifelines but Eveliina, his Finnish girlfriend from another missionary family in Africa. Convinced that every other soul on the planet misunderstood him, he bolted back to America, alone, homeless, and destitute.

"It's a snowball effect. It gets so out of control you're just trying to keep your head above water. You don't really know what you're doing. You don't know how you got there. You're in situations where you weigh what's happening against what you were taught, and you're like, 'What happened? How did I get here?'"

A restaurant job offered a brief attempt at normalcy, but it ended with Blue scrounging for food in the dumpster for the first time. He fell into a lifestyle of drug use, drug sales, and more brushes with death. Thugs wielding machine guns robbed the crack house where he stayed. His own use of booze and marijuana spiraled into harder stuff—cocaine, speed, crack, and crystal meth. He sold drugs just to eat.

Garbage in, garbage out. Blue's heart and hands were as filthy as the dumpsters from which he ate.

Laying Down the Cross

Throughout the long two years Blue was homeless, he checked in with Eveliina, his one connection with a life that delighted in the law of the Lord. Then he would hang up the phone and dive back into the mire.

And deeper he dived. Blue rode along during the gang ritual of drive-by shootings. His appetite for such violence waned almost as soon as it began, however, and he and best friend, Anthony, made a pact never to take the risk again. Blue hustled up enough money to travel to Finland to visit Eveliina. When he arrived in Finland, he received a call. Anthony had broken the promise. Police arrested him after another drive-by, and he remains in prison today.

When Blue returned to Georgia, he stayed away from violence but faded further into drugs. He lived in a chemical haze for days on end, and in one of those stupors he had sex with a girl from whom he had bought drugs. Eveliina flew in from Finland shortly afterward and learned the news from one of Blue's friends.

Blue watched Eveliina reach for a phone to call her father back in Finland. He had shattered another heart and severed his last lifeline.

"She was the only reason for living, which is sad that God couldn't be. I guess it was because she was physical, she was flesh," Blue said.

The cauldron inside finally spewed. Blue told someone he planned to kill the friend who had shared the news with Eveliina. Blue sat in a stairwell, calmly tied his shoelaces, and took the gold cross from around his neck and laid it by his side. Then he grabbed a beer bottle, smashed it, and lunged toward his nemesis.

At struggle's end, the friend-turned-nemesis held Blue from behind, hysterical and sobbing that Blue had tried to gut him. Rattled by the crying, Blue took off into a wooded area. He yanked off his long belt that had gang writing on it, threw it over a tree limb, and wrapped it around his neck. He screamed an invitation for the friend he'd tried to kill to come and watch him die. Then he looked up to see a startled Eveliina, who had followed him.

"I said, 'Babe, it's over. You've already said you're leaving. Just go.' Another guy told her, 'Go call 911.' We're over in the hood. She goes to someone's door and calls 911," Blue said. "I remember saying, 'This is it.' I put my feet up against the tree and stepped out as far as I could and started choking myself. My vision started fading. Life almost looked like a painting.

"But the guy who told Eveliina to call 911 came and jumped on top of me and pulled me down, and I lay there on my back and looked at the sky. I was like, 'God, what am I doing with my life? How did I get to this point?' No matter how far into this thing I went, it didn't end. You never hit rock bottom with sin. You might hit rock bottom with depression, but the spiritual world is infinite in both directions, I guess. The more you want to know God, the more you can know God and will know God. The more you want sin, the further it'll take you until it becomes death. At that point, it was death.

"Lying there on my back, I really felt I was dying. I was ready to die."

CHAPTER 3

STUCK

Somewhere in the Middle / The Altar and the Door

With eyes wide open to the differences
The God we want and the God who is
But will we trade our dreams for his
Or are we caught in the middle?

My co-pastor Reagan Farris and I were at work several years ago when one of our students dropped by. As we prepared for the Wednesday night's youth group worship hour called Refuge, our student introduced us to a whole new world.

"You need to go to *MySpace.com* and see what's going on," the student said.

MySpace had just hit the schools, and the hallways were buzzing with this addictive new site that pulled back the curtains on the lives of people, mostly students, all over the world. Before long, we briefed our senior pastor Tim Dowdy, and he joined our disheartening trek through the cybersludge.

We spent many hours weaving through the tangled webs of our students, tracing "friends" pages for miles. One click led to another, which led to another, each page revealing the surprising connections of an otherwise detached generation. The candor of these kids surprised me. They posted revealing descriptions of their lives.

They also posted the movies they love (some of which would turn their parents' faces red), the songs they sing (including some with explicit lyrics that require earplugs), and the places they go — some dark and even deadly.

Their photos revealed questionable activities with other MySpace friends, all smiling, arms around each other, the world their sin-baked oyster. These students belonged to our youth group, the same ones who stood in worship and bowed their heads in prayer each week.

They didn't realize it, but they were stuck somewhere in the middle. They were caught between the hot and the cold, the new and the old. Somewhere between the wrong and the right, the darkness and the light.

"You know what, Reagan?" I asked. "We're looking at teenagers who are living different lives when they walk in these church doors from the ones they're living away from here."

It's sad how well kids emulate adults.

Lukewarm

The slow fade can often pick up steam and dump us in the muddled middle, where believers are neutralized by their choices and often bear a striking resemblance to the world they are supposed to change. The muddled middle is where Christians earn the tag of "hypocrite," a status Jesus describes when he addresses the seven churches in the last book of the Bible.

In Revelation 2:1 – 5, Jesus commends the church at Ephesus for her many efforts but warns her of failure in a more critical area. She has lost her first love. He tells her to remember how far she has fallen, to repent, and to return to her first works as a demonstration of her primary devotion — in other words, to focus on Jesus himself rather than on the works.

One chapter later, Jesus' language is even more frank in his letter to the church in Laodicea:

> "I know your works: you are neither cold nor hot. Would that you were either cold or hot! So, because you are lukewarm, and neither hot nor cold, I will spit you out of my mouth. For you say, I am rich, I have prospered, and I need nothing, not realiz-

ing that you are wretched, pitiable, poor,
blind, and naked.... Those whom I love, I
reprove and discipline, so be zealous and
repent."

REVELATION 3:15–17, 19

I remember some of the water fountains at my elementary school. I'd come in from recess, sweat streaking my face and matting my hair, dying for a long drink of cold water — only to find that a broken compressor had left the water tepid. Few experiences are more unsatisfying than slurping from a lukewarm water supply.

Jesus uses this vivid word picture to describe the lack of passion and effectiveness of saints who are fence sitters. Remember, he is writing to the *church* in Laodicea. They want both Jesus *and* the world — but it doesn't work like that. "Quit pretending," Jesus says. "This gap between what you say and how you live makes me want to spit you out."

Hitting Close to Home

Nobody walks out of church wanting to fail. Nobody wants to compromise. We trip and fall because life is hard. The world confronting us is fallen, broken, and decimated by sin. It is controlled by the prince of the power of the air, Satan himself.

There's no way we can make it without our own Jesus.

The believer without a meaningful and practiced walk with Jesus and without a deep-rooted support system is a believer susceptible to the world's sway. The slow fade takes that believer far away from her anchor and leaves her somewhere in the middle, somewhere between the altar of her faith and the door of living out that faith.

The same believers who have such powerful feelings of peace as they worship in a gathering of other believers are not always surrounded by encouragement outside their safe havens. Sometimes even their homes are battlegrounds. It's a terrible thing to be so challenged and overwhelmed, to be befuddled believers in the hands of an angry world.

It's crucial to recognize this tension. In fact, I often find myself meandering somewhere in the middle, just beyond the range of usefulness. It is where, I have to admit, I am trained well beyond my obedience.

Paul understood this. He told the Philippians, "Let us hold true to what we have attained. Brothers, join in imitating me, and keep your eyes on those who walk according to the example you have in us" (3:16–17). He implores us to live what we know to be true in God's Word.

If you're like me, you tend to equate spiritual depth with learning something new and profound. But God equates spiritual depth with *obedience*. Paul tells us to live up to what we've already attained, adhering to the elementary principles of the faith. Keep adhering and keep growing. Such a life demonstrates that it is transformed and, because of that, is transformative.

Sitting in the Middle

Psalm 1 describes the descent from walking to standing to sitting — to being stuck somewhere in the middle. The sitting believer is a jaded believer. He's ambivalent and often bitter. Perhaps something didn't go his way, and he's mad. His only hope is for Jesus to break through his thickness with a moment of realization — the kind of awakening that came to the prodigal son, of whom Luke writes, "He came to himself" (Luke 15:17).

Some people spend years in this stage of realizing they're wrong, yet do nothing about it. The prodigal said, "Man, my dad's servants are better off than I am." He dreaded having to swallow his pride and head back home, but still *he responded*. The moment we realize "I used to be closer to God than I am right now" is the moment we realize we're stuck somewhere in the middle.

The most miserable person on the planet is a believer who is running from God, because the Holy Spirit lives in the believer. The Spirit says, "I am going this way. I'm pointing to Jesus." As we try to run the other way, we feel the incredible tension and dissatisfaction of being pulled in two directions. When we get off course, the Holy Spirit will respond, "No, let's go this way. Over here. This way." We can grieve him and follow detours and distractions all we want—we can get our lives as loud and as busy as possible—but every time it gets quiet, the Holy Spirit will be right there whispering, "You're supposed to be over here."

We all have our moments of regret when we walk into our church and think, "I should be so much closer to Jesus than I am." I don't *want* to grieve God, but I do. But usually I can't let others know. I can't be transparent and honest. Instead, I'd rather throw around my Christian lingo and become a fearless warrior behind a picket fence. I'd rather take the lead with reckless abandon, as long as it's wrapped in common sense. I'd rather tell you about my ocean-deep faith, as long as I can tell you about it from the wading pool.

We Christians are amazingly bold when and where it doesn't matter. It's easy to yell "Glory!" in an arena full of believers during a Casting Crowns concert, but the truth is that it doesn't matter to anybody else that a roomful of people are shouting. We're not making a difference to anybody in Kenya, where our students go on a mission trip every year, or on the Pine Ridge Indian Reservation in South Dakota, where our church sent more than a hundred people to minister to the Lakota Indians during spring break in 2009. These people don't hear us being bold in a concert hall.

Of course, we need such moments, but we need *more* than those moments. How much of that boldness even makes it to the car with us after the concert, much less to work or school? And we ask, "Just how close can I get, Lord, to my surrender without losing all control?"

The God We Want

I've learned a sobering fact: My problem is *me*. I get in God's way. The difference between where I am with the Lord and where I should be is the difference between the God I want and the God who is.

It's amazing to discover that God has dreams for us, but it's hard when we realize that our dreams and God's dreams aren't always the same. And it's a tragedy when we go our own way rather than God's.

When we're caught in the middle, we focus on ourselves. We grow callous to the things of God. We live for Numero Uno. We tuck our sticky, gooey hands in our pockets so that no one can see or touch them, and we play it cool. Life on our terms. Perhaps we cast an occasional glance toward God, but we dare not hold our stare because of the discomfort it brings. Only the god we *want* gives us the kind of comfort we want.

The God who *is*? He's different. He's terribly inconvenient.

In Luke 18:18−30, we meet a rich young ruler who didn't know God. He is a telling example for everyone, even believers, who fall into the trap of wanting a life based on personal preference rather than on God's perfect precepts.

Jesus had departed from Galilee for Judea, most likely to places north of Jerusalem and on the eastern side of the Jordan River. Hundreds of sick, diseased, paralyzed, and deformed people found him there, and he healed them all. Word spread, and the Pharisees trudged across the hilly terrain and the river to find him and to test him.

Then up walked a young man who was probably in his early thirties. Maybe he had inherited great wealth or built a successful business. The common assumption was that a man of his stature would sail through the requirements for heaven. First-century Jews believed personal wealth meant God had lavished his favor on that person. His money proved God accepted him.

This young man addressed Jesus as "Good Teacher" and asked what he must do to inherit eternal life. He was willing to say anything to make a pious impression. Instead, Jesus answered his question with a question. "Why do you call me good? No one is good except God alone." In an instant, Jesus had set the agenda. *Only God is good—the rest are sinners.*

Jesus knew the young man didn't get it, so he used the man's own logic to unveil his spiritual bankruptcy. The man fancied himself a do-gooder and assumed he could get by on works and temple sacrifices.

Jesus told him he could have eternal life by keeping the commandments, the Old Testament law. In other words, Jesus told him to live a perfect life. Galatians 3:24 tells us that God gave the law as a tutor to lead us to Christ. The law demonstrates the impossibility of living a sinless life and underlines our need for a sinless Savior.

"Commandments?" the rich young ruler asked. "Which ones?"

Jesus went down a list. Don't kill anybody. Don't commit adultery. Don't steal. Don't lie. Honor your parents. Matthew's account of this story says that Jesus even threw in the second part of the Greatest Commandment: Love others as much as you love yourself (Matthew 19:19).

The rich young ruler reacted just as I would have. Clueless and consumed with self, he looked at Jesus with a straight face and said, "I've kept all of those standards my entire life. What else do I need to do?"

The guy considered himself perfect. Now Jesus had the man where he wanted him and zeroed in on the one issue that would keep the man from faith. "If you want to be perfect," Jesus said, "sell all that you have and distribute to the poor, and you will have treasure in heaven; and come, follow me" (Luke 18:22).

The young man went away sorrowful, unwilling to give up his great possessions. He had stood before the God who is.

And he traded him for the god he wanted.

The Strain

It's easy to assume that if Jesus ever stood before us in the flesh, we'd have the spiritual sensibility to recognize him for who he is and surrender to him. But I know myself. I'd act just like the rich young ruler, who saw Jesus in person. And I have something he never had—God's perfect and proven Word. Yet I *still* don't always recognize Jesus as Lord over my whole life.

It all comes down to the tension between the god we want and the God who is.

The god we *want* fills our belly; the God who *is* fills us with the Holy Spirit. The god we *want* is happy in the middle; the God who *is* reigns from on high. The god we *want* looks a lot like us; the God who *is* wants us to be a reflection of him.

The god we want shows up in comfortable non-verses that we assume are in the Bible but really aren't. *God helps those who help themselves. God blesses the rich so they can bless others. God won't give you anything you can't handle.* These "verses" describe the god we *wish* we had, rather than the God who *is*.

What will the real God do? He'll put us out in the middle of a sea and tell us to walk on it. He'll place us before a giant with a rock and a sling. He'll allow a tornado or cancer or a heart attack or a foreclosure or a job loss or a death to come our way. He will give us more than we can handle just to show us that *only he can handle things*.

When I'm not in his Word, hungering after my own Jesus, I don't understand the God who is. Instead, I assume that God looks the way I want him to look and uses my kind of logic.

Customized Boxes

Where are we in our walk with Jesus? Do we each have our own Jesus? Or are we stuck somewhere in the middle? Do we worship the god we want or the God who is?

Is God a personal Santa Claus waiting to lavish gifts? Is he a genie in a bottle, ready to grant wishes? Or is he the old, sweet grandfather who says, "Everything's gonna be OK. I know you messed up, but you're only human, after all." Or maybe he's like Darth Vader, waiting to choke us with the two-finger Force Grip at the first sign of failure.

So much of our personal theology is built around our personalities, our passions, and our spiritual gifts. We resort to inventing a god that justifies the way we already live and think. It's really not authentic theology as much as personal preference: "This is what I'm comfortable with, and I found a verse for it." That's all the justification we need sometimes, regardless of whether the context of the Scripture is speaking to the situation.

People with a gift of prophecy will see a God who is vocal, while people with a gift of administration will see a God who really cares about the church calendar. This is why the church is called a body, and why God intends all the parts to work together.

When the rich young ruler walked up to Jesus and said, "What must I do to live forever?" he was ready to follow Jesus for life. He just wasn't ready to hear what Jesus actually said. He had a breaking point, an untouchable category in his life that he wouldn't allow anyone else to control. That's why he went away sorrowful and silent. He didn't have anything to say, because he already had the god he wanted — and he could take that god home in a box.

God is too big for our personal boxes. The goal is to be so intimate with Jesus that we know without hesitation the truth of who he is, what he's done, and what lengths he will go to for his children. The goal is to allow the God who *is* to reign over *every part* of our lives and not just the parts where we're already feeling comfortable.

The goal is for Jesus to look at our hearts and say, "That's *my* space."

Jesus, Anyone?

Even when we grasp the truth of the God who is, we often face another challenge. It's not enough to know truth; we have to live it.

When I was fourteen years old, my dad decided to

teach me how to play tennis. We puttered around the local courts, more sincere than graceful, but I showed enough promise that Dad pulled out his wallet and invested more than just himself in me.

Looking back, I realize how much he sacrificed to pay for my tennis lessons. We weren't rich, and I hadn't exactly convinced him I was the next Boris Becker (a big name back in the day). He just wanted to encourage me in one of my interests.

I had a cool dad.

The nearest place for tennis lessons was a ritzy country club, yet Dad footed the bill anyway. I shuffled onto the court to meet my new coach, a little self-conscious because I knew I was in high cotton. Out walked this little guy who looked like Panama Jack (another big name back then). He had the wide-brimmed hat and scruffy beard. Tight white shorts rode high on his thighs, showing off more leg than KFC at lunchtime.

Coach Mann stood only a few inches taller than me. I looked at him and twirled my racket, muttering to myself, "What can *this* little guy do?"

I still didn't know the answer by the third lesson. My first two sessions covered the correct grip on the racket, which felt horribly unnatural, and the most effective way to hit a backhand return, which felt even worse.

"I want you to turn your racket sideways," said my

coach in a low, steady voice, "and I want you to keep the head of the racket parallel to the ground all the way down. The face of the racket should be open to the ground rather than open to the ball."

I muttered to myself some more.

Coach Mann drilled on. I wouldn't have felt more contorted had I been playing Twister. I flashed back to grade school pictures: "Lean forward, cock your head to the right, push your chin out a little bit, turn so your ears are a tad more this way. Now smile and look natural."

I looked like a natural idiot.

I listened to Coach Mann for one reason: my dad's wallet. I didn't want to disappoint, so I followed instructions even through my doubts. I still had never seen Coach Mann *do* anything. He was just some guy who pushed a shopping cart full of tennis balls that he relished throwing at me while yelling at me to twist into the oddest positions. At one point I thought, "Are you standing in for the guy who's supposed to be teaching me?"

As anyone who has played organized sports knows, a coach must first uncoach. He has to break bad habits and techniques, however effective they might be in the short term, in order to make greater success possible in the long term. In basketball, you might fling the ball from behind your head with both hands, make a few baskets, and think, "This must be OK." But trust me, it's not.

In tennis, I had my little swatty way of hitting a ball, and I didn't always lose a match. The occasional victory over an equally hapless friend made me think I was doing *something* right—until I plodded through Coach Mann's goofy methods, which I couldn't seem to master.

Shortly after beginning my lessons, I played against some friends. Did I rely on Coach Mann's techniques? No. Out of habit, I reverted to my old moves. I didn't believe his advice would work on the court because I'd never seen it all come together.

Then one day he showed me what "all together" looks like.

Coach Mann *finally* went to the opposite side of the net and hit some balls with me. Have you ever seen a cat toy with a mouse? I honestly don't think he ever left the center of the court, but he ran me all over the joint. No matter what I did or how hard I hit it, the ball always went right back to him, and he kept running me around, pummeling me.

Sweat dripped from my chin; he was drier than his humor.

I started thinking, "OK, I'm going to listen to this

guy." After his display of skill, I would've held the racket upside down and hit blindfolded if he'd asked *because I'd seen his advice working in the real world.*

All that remained was for me to discipline myself in his techniques and work them into my game instead of relying on my old habits.

A Serious Disconnect

Coach Mann upped the ante. He paired me with other guys who had been taking lessons for weeks and months longer than I had. I noticed how they were executing Coach's techniques and had another epiphany. His other students actually made it happen. Little guys could play the right way too. It dawned on me that I was going to improve only if I worked at the new stuff and tried it in a game where it counted. Until I did, I would suffer a disconnect between me in my tennis lessons and me in an actual game.

Sound familiar?

I see the same kind of contrast in my walk with Jesus.

It's the difference between me at my desk with my Bible open and later in the day insisting on my way in a disagreement. It's me on my knees praying versus my traffic-jam utterances when I'm late for a meeting. It's me serving at an orphanage in Kenya and returning home to whine about the scuffed paint in my house.

When I see the difference between the person I'm called to be and the person I am, I can only fling up my hands and ask, "What's the *deal*?"

I come to church and worship the Lord — and life is beautiful. I'm on the same page with my brothers and sisters and with God. I know where I'm headed. I'm full of purpose. Everything is black and white, and I know right from wrong. Sin reeks when I'm at the altar. I know what I need to lay down. I know what I need to pick up.

And then, somewhere between the altar and the door, everything falls apart. I slip out the door into the world, and it's as if everything I thought and felt and committed to sinks into a black hole.

The song I wrote called "The Altar and the Door" came from such personal experiences: *"But this time, Jesus, how can I be sure that I will not lose my follow-through between the altar and the door?"*

The question frames our predicament. The place between the altar and the door is the place of follow-through — or lack thereof. It's a place of choice, where we either commit to follow what we know to be truth or we chase our own ideas.

Game, Set, Match?

To get better at tennis, I needed to break a few comfortable habits and try something unnatural. But it felt unnatural only because it was new, not because it was wrong. I had never tried it in a game.

I'll never forget the first time I attempted my new backhand swing in a match. I challenged my buddy Rex Harrell. We snuck onto the forbidden courts at a neighborhood apartment complex, and Rex lined up to serve. Just wide right—fault!

I faced his second serve, knowing it would track a little softer. I thought, "It's going to go to my backhand side, and I'm going to try this new shot." He served, and I twisted just as I had been coached—dropping my shoulder, pivoting through the crazy, contorted motion, reaching back and ...

Wham!

The meanest, fastest shot my puny sinews had ever produced rocketed cross court—inside the line—and stuck in the back fence. Rex almost fell trying to reach it. I don't know whose eyebrows arched higher, my buddy's or mine.

"Oh my goodness!" I thought. "Coach Mann is a genius!"

Rex served again, and I tried the shot again ...

And screwed it up.

I tried again a few minutes later and totally blew it. I tried again. Failure.

I lost.

Hollywood endings aren't so common in real life.

But I learned something that keeps on helping me every day, especially in my walk with Jesus. I thought, "All right, do I want to beat Rex right now and win just a few matches every now and then, or do I really want to get good at this so I can win consistently?"

From then on, I hung on Panama Jack's every word.

Follow-Through

Applying tennis lessons is one thing; applying biblical principles is quite another.

I can walk with God in the locker room of church services, small group times, and even personal quiet times. I can walk with God in practices and drills, where I'm feeling safe around other Christians. But if I've never done it out in the world, where consequences loom, then I've never truly walked with God.

Truth is, the Lord didn't save me just so I could rub

shoulders with other Christians, but so I could be his hands and heart in a hurting world. Have I truly accepted this idea? Or am I content to sit on the sidelines?

The first truth about compromise is this: It starts in our minds. Even the tiniest compromise begins with a fracture between Jesus and us. The apostle Paul revealed that he sometimes rose from his knees, walked out into the world, and blew it. "I do not understand my own actions. For I do not do what I want, but I do the very thing I hate.... For I have the desire to do what is right, but not the ability to carry it out" (Romans 7:15, 18).

Paul points the finger at the presence of sin in him. He desires to do what is right but doesn't have the ability to follow through. My eyes widen a little on that one. We're talking about the greatest evangelist, next to Jesus, the world has ever seen, and he admits that he can't control himself.

Paul can't control himself.

Paul suggests a solution, however. Romans 8 is one of the most beautiful portions of literature ever created, and it states without equivocation that while *we* can't overcome sin ourselves, Christ in us most certainly can:

> Therefore, there is now no condemnation for those who are in Christ Jesus,

because through Christ Jesus the law of the
Spirit of life set me free from the law of sin
and death....

You, however, are controlled not by the
sinful nature but by the Spirit, if the Spirit
of God lives in you.

ROMANS 8:1–2, 9 NIV

Two chapters earlier, Paul says we died to sin when
we accepted Christ (Romans 6:2). This truth is hard
to grasp, much harder than a funky grip on a tennis
racket. However, the heart of our faith is faith itself. We
can choose to believe God's Word and respond accord-
ingly, or we can continue living in the muted middle,
with its overcast skies, hazy horizons, and 100 percent
chance of discontent.

Nuts and Bolts

Paul wraps up that famous passage in Romans 7 by
writing, "Wretched man that I am! Who will deliver me
from this body of death?" (Romans 7:24). Some theolo-
gians argue he is speaking hypothetically or referring
to his pre-salvation days. These suggestions set Paul
up to be superhuman and incapable of such sentiments

after salvation. But I believe it's more accurate to let Scripture say what it says—and it says that Paul mirrored you and me.

He struggled his Tarsus off.

Speaking to himself as well, he addresses believers in his letter to the Galatians.

> I say then: Walk in the Spirit, and you
> shall not fulfill the lust of the flesh. For the
> flesh lusts against the Spirit, and the Spirit
> against the flesh; and these are contrary
> to one another, so that you do not do the
> things that you wish.
>
> GALATIANS 5:16–17 NKJV

Sounds like a remedy for the cancer of compromise: *walk in the Spirit.*

Walking in the Spirit means a daily nuts-and-bolts, fundamental, just-do-it pursuit of intimacy with the Lover and Creator of your soul. I cannot stress enough that much of your walk with Jesus is volitional—the result of a decision of the will. Yes, we are talking post-salvation. Jesus alone is responsible for your salvation. But a faithful walk with him consists of one decision of obedience after another.

Have I responded to that clear nudging to
witness to someone?

Have I taken a stand when my colleague
wants to take a shortcut?

Do I live in such a way that my attitudes
and actions testify to the love of Jesus
just as loudly as my lips?

Have I denied myself and loved "the least of
these" (Matthew 25:40) as Jesus did?

Until I choose to follow God's leading and obey him
daily no matter what, this kind of abandonment will
seem like nothing more than a foreign notion.

The Holey Grail

One reason we compromise is we don't know our Savior well enough. Who is Jesus? For many people in the church, he is little more than a Sunday morning worship service. He's just words on a screen. Notes in a conference binder. Jesus is youth camp emotion, weekend retreat resolve, or a daily devotional book. I see it all the time in adults and young people.

Often we believe that chasing rules and fulfilling regimens equate to friendship with God. But when we slip and fall, God disappears. If Jesus doesn't become a person to us—a friend who sticks with us no matter what—then the closest we'll ever get to God is empty religion.

Religion is the holey grail—a cup with a hole in it. It never fills us. We have to keep going back because religion stays in the sanctuary. That's why we find ourselves doing great when we're there and not so great when we're somewhere else.

When we're caught in the cycle of compromise, we can become guilt-ridden and try and try to do our best. We feel we have to do something, anything, to pacify an angry God, so we sometimes substitute ritual for relationship. We're trying religiously to earn God's favor, never realizing that Jesus is already standing beside us.

If we feel secure in the Christian life only when we're at church, then we've signed up for Big Group Jesus.

Big Group Jesus is what I call the weird phenomenon when a bunch of believers get together, and the music and preaching are just right. It gets louder, the emotion intensifies, and the people sing and respond with more passion. Half of them don't even know why they're doing it, but they're having a vicarious experience through the authentic worship of others. For many, it's just that—an experience going on around them—and they're seeing and feeling the effects of it. But it's not in their hearts.

Unfortunately, group worship is as close to God as many of them have ever been, so they figure, "This must be who God is. I need to stay around this stuff. If I leave the building, these feelings will disappear." This is what happens when we don't have our own Jesus.

It reminds me of a teenager trying to figure out what love means. She has a crush on someone, so she decides she's "in love." Her affection is the most extreme feeling she has experienced in her young life. That alone registers with her immature mind and body. *I've never felt this strongly about anything before. This must be love.* What she doesn't know is that there are other, deeper feelings and thoughts she has yet to experience.

In the same way, Big Group Jesus moments send the baby believer chasing his tail, because the church experience never goes home with him. When he walks out the door and into the world, it disappears. He doesn't know a person—he only knows a religious experience that fades over time.

There is a huge difference between Big Group Jesus and real fellowship with God. I always tell people at our concerts that the neat feelings they experience during our worship time won't make it to the parking lot with them. By the time they're loading up the car, they're already trying to get the kids buckled up and fretting about the traffic while a million other thoughts and concerns cloud their minds.

Two miles later, they're left wondering what happened between the altar and the door.

What about you? Your own Jesus — and no one else's — should go home with you when the night is over. Your own Jesus should have gone with you in the first place. If your own Jesus isn't with you, it won't be long until Satan finally convinces you ...

"This must be all there is to a walk with God, and it's not really working."

Accountability

When I was a teenager, looking at porn required serious bravery. You had to walk into a store, go to a section you had no business browsing, grab a dirty magazine, and walk up to a register — behind which stood an adult clerk. Fortunately, I was the biggest coward on the planet. I never had the guts to try.

But that doesn't mean I never looked at it.

My parents screened my television watching. So I just went to a friend's house. My friend had HBO. I learned quickly that it was fun to spend the night at

Billy's house on Friday nights. My eyes were opened to a whole new world.

I'm thankful I only experimented a little. As I grew older, I wasn't around pornography much, encountering the occasional racy scene in a movie. God shielded me and kept it from mushrooming into a bigger issue.

When I became an adult, I appreciated God's protection even more. One day while serving as a young student pastor at Center Hill Baptist Church in Loganville, Georgia, I heard someone else on the staff mention the possibility of bringing Internet service into the church. I said, "The Internet? That's awesome! If we had the Internet, we could do so much. We could do research and learn from other churches. We could market our church." I saw it as a tool. Smutty images didn't enter my mind. I had no idea that 420 million pages of porn littered the Internet.

I talked the staff into going online. Two days after installation, one of my fellow pastors screamed from his office.

"Mark! Come in here! Come in here right now! Come in here right now!"

I thought his hair had caught fire or something. I bolted to his office only to see him sitting at his desk, both hands in the air, staring at his computer screen.

"I do *not* know where this came from. I did *not* click on this site on purpose."

I saw nothing but a blank screen. In a panic, he had shut off his monitor.

"What happened?" I asked.

"Man, all I typed in was the word *weather.* That's all I typed in," he said. "I don't know how or why this other page came up." At that moment, we knew life had changed. Suddenly, viewing pornography didn't require slinking into a store or visiting a friend; it required a mere click on a website link. And it scared me to death.

Our staff waged war on the Internet. I installed an accountability program to block even the slightest chance I would stray to an unintended site. I talked to the staff about it, because in my mind I had brought this monster into the church. Since then, I've always had some sort of accountability on the computer, because I don't need *that* kind of freedom in my life.

Two Battles

I call this kind of approach the battle of the heart and the battle of the hands. We must fight to carry our follow-through from the altar out the door and into the world. The battles are constant because we'll always face temptation and an enemy named Satan.

I have a mantra: *In the war of the mind I must make my stand, with the battle of the heart and the battle of the hands.*

The battle of the heart means we should live lives of worship simply because we love Jesus.

Our lives should be a response to what Jesus has done and how awesome he is. Guarding my heart by guarding my time with God every day makes me a different person. When I'm a Psalm 1 guy, delighting in the law of the Lord, I see other people, the world, and temptation in a different light.

Jesus is all about the motivation behind my actions, and his Holy Spirit and Word gauge my motives. Think of the Sermon on the Mount. If I'm going to give, I should do it for the right reasons; if I'm going to pray, I should do it for the right reasons. If I'm doing it to be seen, I'm wasting my time. Motives are the core of the battle of the heart. When I draw close to the Lord, I surrender more and more to the control of his Holy Spirit within me, which is the definition of being Spirit-filled. This is how to win the battle of the heart on a daily basis.

The battle of the hands results from the reality that

my heart is not always where it should be on a daily basis.

I'm an ebb-and-flow kind of guy. I'm on fire for the Lord, and then I cool. Back and forth. If I act based only on my heart, I could be in trouble. This is why I need to establish roadblocks in my life for those days when my heart goes places it shouldn't. These roadblocks stop me from doing something, even if I want to do it—and the next day I'll be grateful I didn't.

I suffered a recent lapse in my daily quiet time. It just went away from me for four or five days, as it often does—mostly because I'm a dork. (I'll be the biggest dork in heaven, for sure.) I had to declare war on myself. I laid my Bible on the pillow and said, "I will not go to bed until I have spent some time in the Word."

Now, shouldn't my heart be in a place where I *hunger* to be in God's Word? Of course. Shouldn't I be so disgusted by the smut on the Internet that I would not even dare think about going there? Yep. But my heart and my flesh love to go their own ways. I've got to install roadblocks for when my heart and flesh go sideways for a moment.

One of the best kinds of roadblocks may be accountability, a commitment that involves real friends in the messiness of our lives.

Tony Nolan is a real friend. He has toured with

Casting Crowns and led thousands of people to the Lord. I've given him the freedom to ask me anything about anything. He can ask me, "What have you been watching on television?" "How are things going on the computer?" "How are your marriage and family life these days?"

I use an Internet-monitoring program called Covenant Eyes (*www.covenanteyes.com*). It automatically emails Tony a log of the sites I visit every week, and I have no control over it.

Recently, I was designing a flier for our Sunday night Bible study groups. I wanted to illustrate it with pictures of high school students. I searched through free images, typing in *students, teens, school, hallway,* and *locker*. Clicking through photo after photo, I couldn't find the right look for my flier. Some photos had poor resolution, some bad color. I plowed ahead.

I clicked on a photo of three girl soccer players. The tiny picture didn't look revealing at all, nor did the other thumbnail photos surrounding it. I saw nothing even close to pornography. But a few of the photos had young ladies in poses a bit too suggestive for my flier. Typical fashion model stuff.

I thought, "Nahhh." And I kept searching.

I didn't know that the photos I had pulled up had come from a website dedicated to sexy women in sports.

I had looked at the thumbnail photos without paying attention to the source website address listed under each image.

Several days after my spiffy flier was finished and distributed, Tony Nolan emailed me:

> Thinking of your song and knowing firsthand the struggle of the flesh, I am starting to think of "The Fade" as an evil bad guy, the villain. All he wants is to subdue you into considering taking a different step other than the righteous one God lays out for us. Like a zombie needing flesh to survive, he too has a voracious appetite for our convictions. And we who are called by God to be front and center in advancing God's kingdom for his glory must utilize our strength to evade THE FADE!
>
> Accountability is one way to do it. I have a few things that came up that we need to check into. There is a website that scored high (on the Covenant Eyes report) and had "sexy women" in the address. Let's EVADE THE FADE!"

Tony's email jarred me. I checked out the Covenant

Eyes report and traced the questionable site back to the day I had worked on the flier for my students. It heartened me to know my accountability software was working and, more important, that my friend cared enough to challenge me as a brother in Christ to keep fighting for victory in the battle of the hands.

All of us have certain areas of weakness. Left to our own strength and wisdom, it's easy to slip. We all need someone we're willing to answer to, someone who doesn't necessarily struggle in the same areas we do but who can give us wisdom. If we don't have somebody who has the freedom to speak truth into our lives, we're in a dangerous place. We need somebody who can ask the hard questions.

Still, much of the battles of the heart and of the hands is personal. My friends won't always be with me, but Jesus will, which is why cultivating a personal walk with him is essential.

It is crucial to have a pastor pour into me, and a worship leader teach me to worship, and a small group leader help me learn to open up—but I still need my own walk with Jesus. Unless I rent a room in my church and never step foot out into the world, those folks aren't going home with me.

If I don't cultivate a dear fellowship with my own Jesus, I'll find myself leaning on everybody else. I'll live off leftovers. And I'll loiter between the altar and the door, doing it my own little swatty way and failing every time to execute the most fundamental maneuver —follow-through.

CHAPTER 4

NEWNESS

The Word Is Alive / Prayer for a Friend

As the rain falls from heaven
Feeds the earth before it returns
Lord, let your Word fall on us
And bring forth the fruit you deserve

He met her at a softball game. From then on, Michael made sure he either arrived early for his games or stayed after playing so he could bump into her. The conversation evolved from cordial to chatty. Before long, the young man had a crush. A lonely heart that had been on the lookout for singles ended up swinging for the fences.

Too bad she was married.

I'll call her Lisa. As Michael's friendship with Lisa grew, he discovered she had separated from her husband. Separated, not divorced. But hearts did what hearts do. He fell for her because he didn't guard himself. Michael played keyboards in our contemporary Christian quartet. I helped found the group while we attended college, and we made pretty good music and great memories.

After Michael began seeing Lisa, the rest of us noticed their blossoming relationship. We mentioned it to Michael a couple of times, but he shrugged us off. We hurt for him because we knew such an improper courtship had no good ending, but Michael kept hanging out with her until they were pretty much dating.

"Well, she's getting divorced," he said. "It's all going to be fine."

It was never fine. It spiraled into a human tragedy with devastating consequences. Lives changed forever.

Michael couldn't see the danger. The other members of the group knew we had to confront him, but we didn't want to judge him. We loved the guy and saw the drawbacks in pursuing a relationship with Lisa, even if she were to fast-track a divorce. Not only was dating her unwise; it wasn't even scriptural (Matthew 19:5−6). We had to tell him the truth. If his friends didn't care enough to try to rescue him, who would?

So we sat down with Michael on the floor at church and talked with him until four in the morning. Michael listened to us but didn't hear us. He endured six hours of pleading and tears, anger and frustration, looked us in the eye, and told us he wasn't leaving Lisa. He continued to see her for the short time needed for her divorce to become final. Then he married her and reaped the whirlwind.

What we didn't know at the time was that Michael, though he was a member of our Christian quartet, wasn't even a Christian.

The Creator God

Do you know who made the heavens and the earth?

Jesus.

Jesus, the Creator-God, has existed from eternity, and he spoke the universe into existence. The apostle John opens his gospel by describing this truth and referring to Jesus as "the Word."

> In the beginning was the Word, and the Word was with God, and the Word was God. He was in the beginning with God. All things were made through him, and without him was not any thing made that was made.
>
> JOHN 1:1−3

The spoken Word of God is living and active (Hebrews 4:12). It is able to pierce to our very core because the Word is the original change agent of all of life and creation. Whatever he says brings life, and whatever he speaks is new. Jesus closes his revealed Word by reminding us, "Behold, I make all things new" (Revelation 21:5 NKJV).

Jesus *always* makes things new.

Paul writes in his letter to the Romans, "For if while we were enemies we were reconciled to God by the death of his Son, much more, now that we are reconciled, shall we be saved by his life" (Romans 5:10). We are spiritually dead without the life of Jesus in us, and his Word feeds this new life within us. The Word of God is our only hope for newness, peace, hope, victory, strength, compassion, forgiveness, grace — for life itself.

Jesus alone can create from nothing.

Jesus alone can transform death into life.

This is a turning point. While compromise leaves us stuck somewhere in the middle and struggling to follow through, we have hope — the wellspring of this hope is newness in God, revealed in the Word of Christ and forged by his Holy Spirit.

This is where God draws a line in the sand. His Word. This is where compromise must stop and obedience must start. For the cycle of spirit-sapping, peace-killing compromise to cease, we must hear and heed the newness of God's life-giving Word. The Holy Spirit first uses it to cleanse our hearts (Romans 1:16–17) and then to transform our minds (Psalm 119:9; Romans 12:2; 2 Timothy 3:16–17).

God's Word transforms by cleansing and making new. It provokes change, leading lost people to salvation and believers to a fresh start.

A Beautiful Thing

Eventually, my friend Michael changed too.

Michael stayed in our group because Lisa had gotten her divorce shortly after our confrontation with him. Then something happened that explained why he hadn't responded to our pleas. Just before Michael and Lisa got married, he surprised me one day as we prepped for our quartet.

"I got saved at church on Sunday," he said. My heart fluttered for a moment as he detailed how God's Word, which he had read and heard preached for years, had moved him to accept Christ a few days earlier.

"Man, I've been praying for you for a long time," I said. "You remember the night we sat down and talked with you about Lisa? I wrote 'Prayer for a Friend' right after that. That song is about you."

That happened in 1995. Michael's story with Lisa

had many twists to come. He admitted he had fooled everyone, including himself, by going to church and playing in our quartet before personally surrendering to Christ. Still, we could only watch him learn the hard way that God forgives and restores but sin still costs. After Michael married her, Lisa had an extramarital affair in which she became pregnant. An already struggling marriage reached its breaking point.

Though Michael's initial poor decision came back to haunt him, God proved once again that he makes all things new. Michael let go of his anger after hearing a sermon on forgiveness. He divorced Lisa but only after staying with her during a lengthy legal process that required a paternity test.

Now, years later, he is serving in the ministry, is happily married, and has children of his own. Michael's life change didn't begin with the divorce; it began when he responded to the gospel just before he got married, enabling him to endure difficult circumstances with grace and graciousness. He knew what newness felt like, so he extended forgiveness and compassion to Lisa.

God is faithful. Each time we fall, he dusts us off. He alone can transform death into life. Newness.

We have to continually ask ourselves where we are in this death spiral called compromise. Sometimes we may need newness so desperately that it will require doing a 180 with our lives.

I'm reminded of the first sermon in the church's history. Three thousand people turned to Jesus when Peter used extensive Scripture quotations to powerfully convey the brand-new truths of the gospel of Christ (Acts 2:14–41). How did the people respond to hearing truth? They were cut to the quick, realized they needed Jesus, and asked, "What shall we do?"

The first word out of Peter's mouth was "Repent" (Acts 2:38).

God's Holy Spirit through his Word does a beautiful thing. He convicts us and draws us within sight of holiness — "amazing grace! how sweet the sound, that saved a wretch like me!" When we are bogged down in our wretchedness, the truth is the plumb line leading us back to God. The sin of compromise is overcome only by the work of the Holy Spirit through his living Word, prompting us, drawing us, inviting us back into communion with our triune God, restoring this relationship for which Jesus died.

Jesus really did die for it. This is serious. We either obey or, frankly, prevail on God's grace and mock the death of Jesus.

Peter could preach because he knew about conviction. Not only had he failed Jesus by denying he knew him, only to be restored (John 18:15–18, 25–27; 21:15–19), but he also remembered a lesson he had learned when Jesus washed his feet (John 13:6–10). Jesus considered Peter "clean," yet Peter still needed a daily cleansing. "The one who has bathed does not need to wash, except for his feet," Jesus said. Through a live illustration, Jesus previewed 1 John 1:9: "If we confess our sins, he is faithful and just to forgive us our sins and to cleanse us from all unrighteousness."

This is heavy stuff, but here's the bottom line: The only way for us to walk in the newness of life is to walk obediently in God's Word. And the only way to walk obediently in God's Word is to know it. As Israel's King David wrote, "The testimony of the LORD is sure, making wise the simple" (Psalm 19:7).

There's no way to fake this. The authenticity of an obedient, transparent walk with God is evident to all. And so is hypocrisy. That's why we need roots that reach deep and wide.

The Junction

Recently, our student ministry at Eagle's Landing went on a ministry trip throughout Georgia and Alabama. We took our student teams—drama, dance, tech, and so on — to five churches to share ideas and encourage each other to use our unique, God-given gifts in ministry. Service is the culmination of God's love and work in our lives. It means we're giving away what God already has given us. There's a reason the Dead Sea is dead even though the vibrant Jordan River empties into it — it has no outlets.

Near Samson, Alabama, sits the tiny town of Geneva, where the Choctawhatchee and Pea Rivers connect at a place called The Junction. Within The Junction is a park, and within that park stands an oak tree.

A serious beast of an oak tree.

The tree is older than the United States of America. It is believed to have stood for more than 350 years. Its trunk is 22 feet wide, and its upper branches reach 75 feet high. Its limbs span 175 feet. The day before our group visited the tree, a local guy offered a little botanical lesson.

"With oak trees, their root system is nearly identical to what you see above the ground," he said. "Their roots reach just as deep as their trunk does and just as wide as their limbs do."

The fellow didn't know it, but he'd just given Reagan Farris and me an awesome devotional thought. The next day, we gathered the students under the behemoth oak.

"Look at this tree. Now, if you could just erase the

ground, what you would see is symmetry. There's just as much going on with those huge roots underground as there is with what you can see above ground," I said. "You've got to grow your roots deep in the Word so that while you're reaching out to the world, you don't fall over. There has to be a balance between what you're doing and what you're soaking in. So, yes, we're here doing ministry, but there are reverse monsters. You could be all about the Word and want to do nothing but study. But if you're not reaching out, like this tree is, you're really not growing. Roots on their own really aren't doing anything.

"At the same time, if all we're about is reaching out and trying to get out into the culture and affect the world and yet we're not making an effort to grow deep roots, we'll fall over when the first storm hits. The entire time you're in ministry, you've got to be rooted in the Word. It goes back to my life verse in Psalm 1. You have to *delight* in the law of the Lord, meditate on it day and night. And just like this oak tree, you'll be planted by streams of living water, nourished and fruitful, time without end."

The poignant example helped our group imagine all of those huge limbs, some as large as normal oak trees, mirrored underground near those two rivers, near those streams of living water.

This is why we each need our own Jesus. The enemy loves to chip away at our root system by challenging our confidence in the Word. He challenges our understanding because so much of our comprehension is only what we've heard from others rather than what we've culled and cultivated through personal study.

We need deep enough *personal* roots in God's Word to combat Satan's gusty lies. The Secret Service doesn't combat counterfeiters by studying their work. Instead, they study the real deal — actual money — so they'll be able to recognize the fake stuff.

Putting the Person in Personal

I once heard pastor and author John Piper say he always has to review his notes when preaching on why the Bible can be trusted because he forgets all of the apologetic facts. Those facts don't hold his faith together, he said. Instead, his faith is built on the roots he has in his walk with Christ through God's Word.

What he said stuck with me. I probably won't ever debate someone into the kingdom. I'm not saying that apologetics aren't useful or that I don't need to deepen my knowledge, but mere facts don't keep me in the

Word. Instead, my relationship and fellowship with my own Jesus blossom into newness of life every day.

Not long ago, I talked with one of my students named Candace. As we discussed spending time with God, a cool word picture came to me. "You know," I said, "the Bible can't be ketchup. The Bible is marinade. You can squirt ketchup on anything you want, and it'll change the food you're eating at that moment. But marinade soaks into the meat and slowly changes the makeup of the meat itself. The meat becomes marinaded. It's a slow process, but it makes a bigger difference."

She smiled. She knows I like food.

"I can't do a ketchup walk with God where I squirt it on every once in a while when I need help or when I'm in trouble or when I need to feel better," I said. "I need a marinade walk."

Marinade saturates by seeping. It penetrates below the surface and changes everything.

I don't have to read the book of James in one sitting. For today, I might need only the first four or five verses of chapter 1. I can prayerfully read until something hits me, and I ask, "God, what are you saying to me through this? Is there a command I need to follow here? Is there an example I need to heed? Is there something I need to lay down? Is there something I need to pick up and use? Is there a promise I need to claim here?"

For instance, if I'm reading the story of the prodigal son, I pray, "God, where am I in this story? Am I the son? Am I running from you? Am I the brother who refuses to forgive someone? Am I bitter and jealous of other people? Am I the dad? Is there someone I need to welcome back and stand with them as they start over?"

Few pursuits please God more than praying his Word back to him.

The letters in the New Testament are instructional. You can pray all the way through them. When the author of an epistle says, "Do this," a proper response is, "God, am I doing this? How can I start? Help me do this." I try to make the moment personal and take his Word personally because I serve a personal God. I want to let it soak into me instead of just squirting it onto my moment.

We shouldn't look at our quiet time — our daily time spent reading the Bible and praying — as something we've *got* to do. It's something we *get* to do. This is a relationship we're growing in, so sharing time with the Lord is not an item to check off our list so we can feel better.

I hear a lot of people say, "I'm doing my quiet time again, and my days are going so much better now." I'm sorry, but their day didn't get a lot better. Their day was just as wonderful or cruddy as it was ever going to be.

What changed was their *perception* of their day. The day wasn't different; they were.

Paul didn't have many good days (see 2 Corinthians 11:21b−28). Think about it: Early in his last letter (2 Timothy), which he wrote to his son in the faith, he says, "Oh, by the way, everyone in the province of Asia has left me. So anyway …" (see 2 Timothy 1:15). And he goes right back to his instruction to Timothy. I wish I could be more like Paul. If a student's mom calls me up and rips into me, it ruins my whole week. Not Paul.

His perception of God changed everything for him.

God doesn't say he'll calm our storms. He might. He might choose to calm our storms, or he might choose to walk through them with us. But the peace that surpasses understanding comes through relationship. It doesn't come from clapping in church or having a lot of Christian friends. It doesn't come from making God in our own image. It comes when we follow through, when we walk out the door ready to trust the Lord in the battle of the heart and the battle of the hands.

A relationship takes quality time. Again, no shortcuts. This is how we grow closer to our own Jesus. This is how we become a giant oak.

Therefore, as you received Christ Jesus
the Lord, so walk in him, rooted and built up

in him and established in the faith, just as you
were taught, abounding in thanksgiving.

COLOSSIANS 2:6–7

Leaving Pleasantville

When you look at the cross section of an oak tree, you
can see it grew different amounts in different seasons.
Growth never happens according to some cold, linear
formula. As the seasons of our lives change, we find opportunities for growth and maturation.

Yet there are also times of contraction, of barren-
ness and disease. One of the great joys of the Christian
life is that we never have to endure such seasons alone.
Our God is always with us, and so too are our brothers and sisters in the body of Christ. When a Christian
stumbles and falls, it is the privilege and the duty of the
church to try to bring restoration.

My bandmates and I didn't know that Michael wasn't
a believer when we confronted him. We just wanted to
obey God's Word and help our friend. I realize now that
valuing others above yourself and putting them first is
a sure barometer of growing in your own Jesus.

The apostle Paul lived for others, abandoning his
comfortable, high-society life for a pauper's gospel. Jesus

so revolutionized Paul's heart that he moved from looking down on the great unwashed to living among them,
and even living below their standards, as he begged
them to give their hearts to God.

Philippians 2:1–4 reveals the difference in Paul as
he puts feet to the Greatest Commandment:

> So if there is any encouragement in
> Christ, any comfort from love, any par-
> ticipation in the Spirit, any affection and
> sympathy, complete my joy by being of the
> same mind, having the same love, being
> in full accord and of one mind. Do noth-
> ing from rivalry or conceit, but in humility
> count others more significant than your-
> selves. Let each of you look not only to his
> own interests, but also to the interests of
> others.

Paul's passion was to nurture Christians into growth in
Christ—and equally to restore them when they fell.

However, confronting a brother or sister in Christ
in order to point them to repentance and restoration
is never easy. Not only is there no guarantee that the
brother or sister will respond; there are also many ways
we can err even as we try to help.

Ultimately, a brother's or sister's obedience to God is more important than our friendship. That is a hard place to land. We don't like tension, conflict, or icky moments. We feel safe in the city limits of Pleasantville. We push things away, suppress reality, and ignore the issue.

Courage is essential, but so is caution. Even when we know we're standing on Scripture and our perspective is the proper one, we never want to come off as self-righteous or holier-than-thou. The path of least resistance is keeping the peace and ignoring God's call to confront a friend. The difficult path is doing what's right and doing it in godliness and love. Despite our fear that we'll stumble over our words or push away our friend or loved one, we can trust that speaking the truth of God's Word into a breaking or broken life—humbly, gently, compassionately—is the best thing we can do.

God has shown me over the years that speaking truth to somebody conveys the message, *I love you. You're my friend. This is what I see happening, and I'm praying for you.*

We can't change people, but God can use us as agents while he changes people—*if* we're willing.

When someone is hurting and walking on a sinful path away from God, that person is probably not happily worshiping beside you in church. That person is already out the door—and if we remain somewhere in the middle, we'll never be able to speak the truth in love. This requires follow-through. It requires walking out the door with a godly heart in order to be God's hands and voice to a friend.

A friend may blow us off, call us names, or laugh in our faces. But later that night, when he's lying in bed staring at the ceiling fan, what's going through his head? He'll be thinking about the truth of what we said—a truth he must deal with sooner or later.

Proverbs 18:24 states, "A man of many companions may come to ruin, but there is a friend who sticks closer than a brother." A true friend resolves to stick closer than a brother. A true friend realizes that only God's grace has protected him from making the same mistakes.

It feels good when we help restore a friend, when we stick closer than a brother. Yet sometimes we must release our friends and loved ones to the Lord—not giving up on them but conceding that God alone can change them. The worst approach is to harass the person you know is in error. Speak truth, do it in love, and live so he or she sees the spoken truth displayed in action.

Harassing God? Now, that's a different matter. Jesus emphasized this point with a parable in Luke 18, teaching believers "always to pray and not lose heart" (verse

1). He told the story of a widow who pestered a judge for justice until the judge, who didn't fear God—much less humans—relented and acted on her behalf. He moved only because of her persistence.

The wrong way to interpret this passage is to presume we can pick up the Bible, skim our favorite passages, bow our heads, rub a spiritual genie bottle, and get what we want as long as we say it often enough. It's tempting to believe we can name something and claim something, and it'll be ours—all because we want it. Just because *we* want it doesn't mean *God* wants it for us. The only name that matters is Jesus' name, and the only claim that matters is the one he has on our lives.

Neither does this parable say that our efforts mean something. It's easy to slip into a works mentality when we read of the dogged efforts of one woman and her positive results. But Jesus didn't stress the works; he zeroed in on the *source* of the works.

The focus of the passage is faith—simple, childlike faith. Why did the lady refuse to quit beseeching the judge? What motivated her? She believed a righteous God ultimately would prevail, somehow, some way, on an unrighteous judge to right a wrong. Her faith drove her works, not the other way around.

What about you? Have you given up?

Have you left a friend for dead, spiritually speaking?

What about one of your children? Are you still faithful every day in your prayers for him or her? Are your prayers formulaic and repetitive? Or are you seeking the mind and heart of the Lord?

The unrighteous judge relented. What will a holy, loving God do in answer to one of his own righteous children?

Christ-Awareness

Remember, we're examining a stage of growth here, a bearing of the fruit of the Spirit (Galatians 5:22 – 23). You can't have love, joy, peace, patience, kindness, goodness, faithfulness, gentleness, and self-control unless Jesus has full control.

In the August 20 entry of *My Utmost for His Highest,* Oswald Chambers points us to one of the most powerful prayers possible: Ask God to replace your self-awareness with Christ-awareness. In other words, we should plead for the mind of Christ in all things. The mind of Christ will put Christ first, and rightfully so. He is God. He is preeminent.

Yet at the same time — and this is the beautiful wonder of following Jesus Christ — the mind of Christ will lead us to serve others.

Jesus didn't give us the Greatest Recommendation; he gave us the Greatest Commandment. He doesn't promise that obedience will be easy. But he promises that it will produce fruit in some way, and he promises to bless those who live within his will (John 15:7–10).

Christ-awareness includes honoring James 5:16 by confessing our trespasses to godly friends and asking them to follow suit. A growing Christian is one who is willing to do the right thing, even when it involves the hard task of confronting someone. Accountability is scary—people don't want someone else rifling through their little compartments. And so it is important for maturing believers to handle confrontation in an appropriate, loving way.

Consider the following warning flares of accountability:

First Warning Flare: It's easy to put on our spiritual robes and cast stones from on high at every little mistake we see others make. In the Sermon on the Mount, Jesus gave us a dipstick to check our oil, and that dipstick takes the shape of a log in the eye (Matthew 7:3–5). He implores us to make sure our lives square with Scripture before we seize our holy rocks.

When facing a potential confrontation with someone, we're supposed to pray a lot more than we talk. That's the time to get on our faces before God. I've heard teachers consistently say that students should study two hours for every hour they spend in class. If that's the case, we need to pray about ten times longer than the time we're going to spend talking with someone as we confront them. It's one of the most serious tests we'll ever face.

We need to check our spirits; we must check our humility. Let's ask God to dissect our attitudes, because we have many motives we are unwilling to confess when confronting people. Sometimes it involves something I call "sin envy": "God, I'm trying my best to live for you, and this person is just out there doing their thing. I'm going to have to help them." Sometimes our confrontational attitude is a cover for our bitterness that the other person gets to have fun sinning, and we don't.

Let me repeat something. *It's more important that this person has a relationship with Jesus than with us.* Let's reach the point where we're willing to say, "I'm laying our friendship on the line here, because this has to be said."

And sometimes within this process of prayer I have discovered God also wanted to change was me.

Second Warning Flare: Be careful not to judge others in areas about which you have no experience or may lack all the information. Coming to oh-so-righteous conclusions after hearing one side of the story is dangerous (Proverbs 18:13, 17).

In a small group Bible study, life can make total sense. A man would never flirt with a married woman after prayer time. But out in the real world, it gets tougher. What about that friendly barista at the coffee shop you see every day? What about a coworker or your boss? Sometimes life blurs and things grow gray. We can choose to nail the sinner to the wall, or we can remember that the sinner's nails have already been used on someone else.

Sometimes we get overzealous about areas outside of our expertise. It's like the ninth-grade girls who come to me and speak judgmentally of the seniors and say, "Well, God told me I'm not going to date until I get married." And all the while I'm thinking, "That could very well be an awesome, biblically based personal conviction. Or it just could be because no one has asked you out yet."

Guarded motivations mean guarded lips. I try to ask myself, "Am I motivated by love, or I am responding like this because I think I'm right?" It helps protect me against being judgmental and reminds me that we're all two or three bad decisions away from destroying ourselves.

Third Warning Flare: One wise tactic when facing a

tough situation is to approach the person with questions rather than statements. If we barge in with pitchforks and torches, we can quickly make an awkward situation even worse. But if we open with questions, then we just might start a conversation. We're giving the person a chance to respond, which affords us an opportunity to provide details about what we have witnessed.

No matter how close the relationship, those who are confronted will invariably look for reasons to discount the persons confronting them. It's human nature. An approach filled with loving questions and transparency is disarming and authentic. If you confront me, it's hard for me to rip you when you admit you've also struggled in a similar area (recall the second warning flare).

Before I approach a friend with questions about something I see in his life, I try to imagine the opposite scenario: What if he confronted me with questions about my behavior?

If you need to confront someone, ask yourself how you would want to be approached. What would you want to hear, and how would you want your friend to say it? You would want to be able to leave the exchange and say, "This person loves me and wants to see God's best in my life." You wouldn't want to leave saying, "This person thinks he's better than I am." Approach is everything.

Remember, at this point you've had days or maybe even weeks to think about how to address your friend. You've spent hours contemplating and praying. Your friend hasn't had that luxury. She is hearing it for the first time and probably will feel as though someone just drove a Mack truck through her living room. You have to be spiritually prepared for her reaction. Chances are it won't include harps and a recitation of Scripture.

Put her first before the moment, and put her first after the moment.

Here's where having your own Jesus comes in again. Your own personal, intimate, practiced walk with God is the only avenue to the wisdom, mercy, and truth you need in your relationships. It's the only way to overcome self, develop Christ-awareness, and place others first.

And it's the only way for people who fail — people like Michael, people like you and me — to live happily ever after.

CHAPTER 5

THE ROMAN SON
Every Man

I am the woman shamed and haunted
By the cry of unborn life
I am every broken man
Nervous child, lonely wife

Barry Riner lay in a pool of blood barely breathing. The gash plunged across the right side of his chest, from his shoulder downward till it stopped in the middle of his diaphragm, severing the wall of muscle designed to assist in breathing.

The breaths were laborious, intermittent. His instincts clung to life, convincing him the air too precious to cry away. The stillness must have been surreal, especially considering he lay in the middle of a hotel room floor on the main strip of an army base town. His twin brother, Larry, lay beside him, an even longer gash carved from the ball of his right shoulder across his front torso to just above his left hip. His wound was almost an evil joke, a cruel sash to commemorate the occasion. *So this is what a world of sin looks like....*

How did the brothers wind up here, now, so soon?

Had their time finally come? Could this be the inglorious end? The brothers were fighters, something they had proved time and again over the previous several months. It wasn't the first time someone tried to kill them, but it was by far the most serious. Maybe all those other times somehow had calloused them for this.

They still had vital signs, each heart sputtering a stubborn cadence, the origin of which only God knows. *Bum-bump, bum-bump, bum-bump.* Their rhythms were palpable and sure but would last only as long as the blood did. The cuts were too long and too deep. No way could they make it, not alone. Barry and Larry's mother lay on the floor, inches away, her head propped against the bed. She appeared unconscious. What kind of person would do all this?

A sudden commotion outside pierced the stillness. A car veered into a parking space near the door. Time was precious. It was 1958, and the only LifeFlight around was on the wings of an angel. Her name was Frances, and she had arrived just in time. The footsteps grew louder, louder, until punctuated by a quick turn of the doorknob and then a gasp that sounded one part astonishment and one part prayer.

That's where the brothers' Aunt Frances found them, coiled on the floor, bleeding, straining for air. She reached down in an instant, ignoring the puddles.

Towels. Get some towels. Did she say that aloud or just think it? Her husband scurried toward the bathroom.

Which one should she attend to first, Barry or Larry? What do you do when your two nephews are bleeding to death right in front of you? Do you freeze, torn which way to go? They were moving, almost imperceptibly, clinging to life as the thickening stain on the floor grew larger by the minute. Which one does a loving aunt choose to help first?

Him. Barry.

Had to be Barry. But why Barry and not Larry?

Aunt Frances reached for Barry first not because she considered his life more precious or his wound more desperate. No, she must have reached for him first for one reason.

She reached for him first because that's what you do to remove the hook of a clothes hanger still lodged in the chest of a ten-inch-long baby ...

Starting Over

Barry Riner grew up in a MoonPie and RC Cola community outside of Atlanta, close enough to the skyscrapers that his little hometown would be considered metro now. It was also far enough away back then that neighbors looked at the big city as something the rest of Georgia just had to put up with.

Barry's parents were as close to Ward and June Cleaver as a full-color life could get, and Barry knew this because the black-and-white television episodes of *Leave it to Beaver* seemed so familiar to him. Sam and Beverly Riner were gentle, quiet, dignified. They were older but fully engaged with their twin boys. It never seemed to dawn on Barry that they were much too old for parenthood.

"I just knew they were my mom and dad, and they loved me very much," Barry said. "I never at any point felt any sense that I didn't belong to them."

Twenty-one years into his idyllic world, Barry answered a phone call that would come just as close to ripping out his heart as that clothes hanger ever did. Larry's voice quivered on the other end of the line. Barry paused from another harried day at his restaurant in downtown Atlanta. It was February 14, 1979 — a Wednesday.

Happy Valentine's Day, buddy.

"I just found out something that's going to blow your mind," Larry said. "It's the worst nightmare I could ever imagine, and I don't even know how to tell you over the phone. But you need to come home right now."

Barely a grown man, Larry already had turned to alcohol. Barry drove to his parents' home, unsure what to expect. Maybe one or both of his parents had died. Or maybe Larry had done something foolish on a drinking binge. Barry arrived to find that his brother's eyes were bloodshot from crying rather than drinking.

"My parents sat down and said, 'This is something we never even prepared for, but we need to tell you. You're not our child. Your biological mother who gave birth to you called this morning. She was drunk, and she told your brother the whole story. We're trying to decide how we're going to deal with this for him because he's not handling it well,'" Barry said. "Through tears, they began telling me the story."

They began telling Barry *his* story:

The little Army town held more soldiers than secrets, and Edith Milton had known plenty of both. Already married several times by 1957, she would eventually marry eight times and give birth to a number of children. Not long after one of her divorces, she married a soldier, who in turn shipped off to Germany, leaving

Edith alone with time, loneliness, and her demons. The evidence suggested the alcohol screamed at her almost as loudly as her need for men. With her husband an ocean away, she succumbed to both.

An adulterous affair with the former husband she had just divorced resulted in another pregnancy. Edith grew more petrified by the ninety-proof ounce. She concocted a simple solution. Before her husband came home in the fall, she would get rid of her problem.

Never mind that there were two problems, side by side, in her womb. Two babies from separate eggs. Fraternal twins.

Edith hit the bottle. Her pickled haze failed to diminish the guilt and instead heightened the fear. Intent on poisoning the two lives inside her, Edith drank a fifth of vodka daily. She got her supply from the bar at which she worked, a well she tapped day after day, week upon week. She had to get rid of the problem. Still, the kicks inside her swelling abdomen grew stronger.

Conscious Decision

The mortifying phone call from soldier boy came in early June. He wouldn't be home in the fall after all; he would be home in mere days.

Edith called her sister, Frances.

"I've got to get rid of these babies because he's coming back," Edith said. "I can't face him with that."

Then the phone went dead.

Frances grabbed her Bible and car keys and looked at her husband. "We've got to find her."

"My aunt said, 'I don't know why, but we went into only one hotel, and it wasn't the first one we came to. We pulled in there, and I saw her car. We went in the door, and she lay on the floor with her head back on the bed,'" Barry said. "I was beside her on the floor, lying in my own blood, and the coat hanger still through my chest. It went in through the right-hand side, just under where my diaphragm would be, and came out through my ribs in the back. In the process, the coat hanger also ripped my brother's front side from his right shoulder diagonally across his torso all the way to just above his left hip. His chest was crushed in. I weighed two pounds and a few ounces. But she wrapped us up and made sure we were breathing, and took the both of us and headed to the hospital."

The calendar read June 7, 1958. Barry Riner recently turned fifty but still has the deep scar on his chest.

Larry, teetering on life's margins already, fell into the abyss. "You lied to me," he told his parents, over and over. The drinking worsened. The family placed him in an advanced alcohol treatment facility for testing. Doctors assessed the positioning of his eyes and determined that he had suffered fetal alcohol syndrome. They offered no scientific reason for why the alcohol affected only Larry in the womb.

Why Larry and not Barry?

Larry's chemical habits descended into drugs. He is behind bars today but built his own prison much earlier. The other son went in the other direction: Barry leaned on Scripture to answer the enemy's taunts and his own questions.

"Paul used the phrase *adoption as sons* over and over in his writings," Barry said. "It was a Roman concept. The Roman Empire apparently had a legal system whereby, if a family adopted a son, that son took the place of the firstborn. He had all the rights and privileges as if he were the first child. Paul described that as the relationship for one who is adopted into God's family.

"I realized that my foster parents got up each day and made a conscious decision to keep us. They were not legally bound to do that. Every morning, they said, 'We'll love them and keep them and take care of them another day,'" Barry said. "I love my three children very much, but I also realize I have a legal obligation. Yet my foster parents could have been free at any moment from that obligation. Maybe it's skewed, but in my way of thinking they had a greater form of love because they continued day by day to recommit themselves to me and to my brother. That strengthened my relationship with them and made me a different person. Unfortunately, my brother always seemed to go back to the question, 'Why weren't we told when we were younger?' That seemed to be the seed Satan took and played with in his case."

A New Name

Dr. Barry Riner now pastors a rural Baptist church in Georgia. His passion for reaching the lost and growing the saved is the spirit behind this step of our cycle.

As we grow in Christ, he broadens our interests. When we are bogged down in compromise, we concentrate on ourselves. Repentance turns us away from ourselves and toward the Lord, who grows us on the upward road to restoration and maturity. Our attention turns more to loved ones and friends, people about whom we naturally care. But ultimately the believer's burden will blossom to Every Man, lost people still wading through the sin muck from which God has rescued us.

This is a wonderful place of maturation in our walk

with our own Jesus. I can't think of a better illustration than Barry Riner.

Nine years ago, God took care of the scar. Not Barry's, but Edith's. Edith's new birth was just as miraculous as Barry's natural one.

On May 14, 2000, Barry preached a sermon titled "Letting Go to Love," based on 1 Kings 3:16–28. It is the account of King Solomon's wisdom in settling a dispute between two harlots, both of whom claimed to be the mother of the same baby boy. Solomon offered to cut the baby in half so that both women could have a share. He knew the real mother would relinquish the child to save him.

"In the process of preaching that sermon I made the statement, 'It is amazing to realize that even a woman whose only means of surviving was by degrading herself as a prostitute, even that mother had the wonderful, remarkable capacity to love enough to give away her child. Probably the only thing she possessed, she gave away,'" Barry said. "Then I gave the invitation."

"Typically, no one responds to the invitation on this annual holiday," Barry said.

"But down the aisle came one woman. It was my biological mother. I did not know she was there, did not see her during the service. She sat in the very back in a row of extra chairs behind the back pew. She came down, and she hugged my neck. She kissed me, and she said, 'I'm sorry. I'm so sorry about what you've gone through.'"

Barry smiled. "I forgive you, Edith. I forgave you a long time ago."

It was a day filled with God's grace and forgiveness, one that left another kind of mark on Barry. It was a day in which the Lord reminded the little boy inside him that his heavenly Father cares enough about him to restore his relationship with the woman who long ago didn't want him. It was a holiday, all right—a special one.

It was Mother's Day.

Edith was in her seventies; Barry was forty-one. All those years. All that pain. So much forgiveness.

"All I know is God looked down the corridors of time and saw that one of those little bloody babies on that floor was going to be a preacher. And what he saw in me I'll never know, but he loved me enough to save me," Barry said. "One of the things that just unnerved me while growing up was to go by a house and see a bunch of junk cars in the driveway. I've changed my philosophy on being offended by that because I married into a family where my wife's grandfather loved old cars, and he would take them and restore them.

"When he died several years ago, I spoke at his funeral and reminded people there that my wife's grandfather was a lot like God, because God doesn't throw away something when it's broken. He takes it in, restores it, and uses it," he said. "I realized that, though I was broken, God restored me and he used me. And though my mother was broken and did some things she has long since regretted, God restored her. Our God restores things. He does not leave us broken. So many of us, if we lose an important part of the collection, we'll get rid of it and sell it on eBay or whatever. God doesn't do that. He likes broken vessels. He restores broken vessels. That's my encouragement."

Every Man is broken and ragged and jaded in this broken and ragged and jaded world. It takes a mature set of eyes to see him as God does.

God Vision

To see people the way Jesus sees them, sometimes we have to climb the highest peaks and plunge to the deepest valleys. Sometimes we have to hit hard bumps and take sharp turns. Sometimes we barrel into the darkness and wonder where we'll end up. Sometimes all we want to do is raise our hands to the heavens, close our eyes, and scream.

Sometimes a roller coaster is involved.

I'm a roller-coaster guy. They're just my thing. I don't do bungee jumping or spinning in circles, but if you strap me to something, you can do pretty much anything you want to do to me. You can drop me off a cliff and shoot me to the center of the earth, and I'm down with it. I'll be holding my hands up all the way.

Since I'm a student pastor, I get a lot of practice. Theme parks are always great places to take students, and I love the bonding time. We spend most of the day waiting in line, and that's one place I really get to know the kids. It's incredible how much quality time I've spent with kids at amusement parks. Sometimes, sad to say, it's the most face time they've had with an adult in years.

When I go to a theme park like Six Flags here in Atlanta, I always pal around with a group of middle schoolers. They're a hoot. High schoolers are a different story. They don't like each other very much, and they go to the bathroom a lot. Too much drama. I hang with middle schoolers because they don't care about anything but vertical height and miles per hour. They'll ride the wildest beast in the park eight times without catching their breath. Their motto is, "We'll eat when we're dead — where's the next ride?"

I went to Six Flags often while on staff at Center Hill Baptist Church in Loganville, Georgia. When I was called to join the staff of First Baptist Church of Daytona Beach, Florida, I realized one big drawback to the move: I had to leave my roller coasters. As Six Flags faded in the rearview mirror, all I could think of were mouse ears and kiddie rides.

One time at Daytona, we planned to take our students to a festival called "Rock the Universe" at Universal Studios in Orlando. Part of Universal Studios is a theme park named Islands of Adventure. I had never been there, but I definitely didn't like its slogan: "Where You Ride the Movies." What does that even mean? Who wants to ride a movie?

But then I saw the roller coasters. They jutted against Orlando's bright blue sky and featured the names of my favorite comic book characters. Maybe this wouldn't be so bad after all.

The Incredible Hulk is a normal roller coaster except for one stark difference. Most roller coasters start out slow, with a gradual climb to the crest of a hill. Anticipation builds during the ascent as you hear *ka-took, ka-took, ka-took, ka-took* while the massive chain underneath lifts you ever higher. It's like a countdown while your mind screams, "What have I done?"

The Incredible Hulk is different. It launches out of the starting gate and shoots up the hill like one of the rockets down the road at Cape Canaveral. As we ripped out of the gate, I threw my hands up and whooped. Welcome to Florida!

But one ride stirred the masses most. *Everyone* wanted to ride Spiderman. Our kids aimed their sights on it early, and I thought, "Cool. Sounds terrific. The Hulk was awesome—how can Spiderman go wrong?"

Then we walked up to Spiderman. It was a building. No tracks. No cars whizzing by with people screaming. Just a building and a gargantuan line. I shook my head and looked at the gang around me. "I don't know that I want to wait three hours to ride a building," I said. "We've got buildings back home. I live in one."

We skipped Spiderman two or three times before the kids finally talked me into it. We waited in line forever, winding back and forth, chatting and laughing and watching people. We reached the building and walked in the doors, thinking we were finally at the ride.

Nope. We'd reached the *inside* line. Now we waited in another queue for almost as long. After what seemed like hours—yes, there *is* such a thing as *too much* quality time in line with middle schoolers—we approached the entrance gates to the ride, and the attendants handed us 3-D glasses. One red lens, one blue.

Now *that* seemed pretty cool. Before long, we sat down, slid on our 3-D glasses, and disappeared into the unknown.

It was the coolest ride I'd ever experienced.

Real fire roared around us while 3-D movies played and building parts fell from above and appeared headed toward us. A loudspeaker system and vibrations in the car jacked up the adrenaline. I screamed in fear and yelled in glee the whole way.

The ride was *almost* perfect.

During the entire ride, a kid behind me did his best to spoil the thrill. Every few seconds, without fail, he blurted out the same thing: "This is duuumb. This is stuuupid." Over and over. In that middle school nasal whine that makes you want to scream. The ride lasted all of two minutes, but he whined the whole way.

"You're clergy, Mark," I told myself. "You can't kill him."

Since I couldn't see him during the ride, I wanted to be sure and take care of business when the ride ended. I wanted to stare him down with one of my patented holier-than-thou glances I give bad drivers on the road. I call it the "No-Nod," a disgusted shake of the head. When we pulled back into the start station, we had enough lighting for me to give the kid a disgruntled look. As I turned in my seat, I discovered that the poor kid had ridden the whole way *without* the 3-D glasses.

Leave it to a middle school boy to wait in line for three hours to go on a 3-D ride, be surrounded by friends and adults wearing 3-D glasses, sit down in a car in which every other person is wearing 3-D glasses — and not wear 3-D glasses. Have you ever seen a 3-D movie without the glasses? It's a giant blur of red and blue.

No wonder he didn't like the ride. For him, it *was* a stupid ride.

That kid reminds me of believers who don't have their own Jesus. Without the intimacy of a one-on-one walk with Jesus, we all walk through life with eyes wide open but blurry vision. We don't have on our spiritual glasses.

In Mark 8, Jesus warns his disciples to guard against the "leaven" of the Pharisees. The disciples had seen their Master's miracles feed thousands of people, so they surmised he was talking about bread again. He wasn't. Jesus was referring to the pervasive hypocrisy of the Pharisaic lifestyle, and he scolded the disciples for being obtuse. "How is it you do not understand?" Jesus asked (Mark 8:21 NKJV).

The disciples proved it was possible to walk in the physical presence of Jesus and still be far from his will. It shouldn't come as a surprise that it's often hard for us to see his will even as we walk with him. How many believers in the church today fail to put on their glasses? They don't get it, they don't see it, and they don't understand it.

With spiritual glasses, you see life differently. You see clearly enough to question yourself: "Whoa. OK, I'm involved over here in ministry at church, and I've been able to keep all of these little interests and pursuits over here separate for a while. But now I don't know if this thing I'm doing out here away from church honors God."

Life changes when you've got your glasses on. You start seeing your life — and the world — as God sees.

Loving the unlovable is a sure sign of having a good pair of glasses. Such compassion comes only from having your own Jesus, a Lord so intimate and powerful that for Barry Riner the scars remained only skin-deep while the love reached into eternity.

Prescription Lenses

When we hear those crying out around us, we often condemn instead of connect because our vision is blurred. When we put on our glasses, we honor the Lord by seeing people not as groups or races or stereotypes but as unique, beautiful, valuable individuals.

When we classify people into groups, it's easier to generalize and get away with it: "Well, people in the South are _____. Baptists are _____. Hispanics are _____. Europeans are _____.

Californians are so stinking _____." If you're like me, you've filled in the blanks more times than you care to admit.

Our spiritual glasses narrow the focus to individual people. Your coworker. Your son's coach. The soldier at the airport. Your daughter's ballet teacher. The man in line at Wal-Mart. It's easier to speak in black and white and put the Jesus smackdown on a group of people. But when a person has a face and a name and a situation, you see things differently. The reason we ask "What would Jesus do?" is that he determined his actions according to what each and every individual he met needed at that time.

I'm not espousing situational theology or ethics. I'm advocating loving 'em like Jesus. There is black and white, right and wrong—and God's Word gives us the only true absolutes. But when we're talking about a group of people, it becomes easy to show an absence of mercy. When we get to specific people, we're much more likely to demonstrate concern.

Most of us realize 2 Corinthians 5:17 teaches if anyone is in Christ, he or she is a new creation—the old has passed away and the new has come. How many of us can put the verse in its context? The apostle Paul wrote it to magnify the ministry of reconciliation, which God initiated by sending Jesus to reconcile us to himself.

Now God expects us to take up the banner. Paul says God is "entrusting to us" this message of reconciliation, a message that reaches one heart at a time.

> Therefore, we are ambassadors for Christ, God making his appeal through us. We implore you on behalf of Christ, be reconciled to God. For our sake he made him to be sin who knew no sin, so that in him we might become the righteousness of God.
>
> 2 Corinthians 5:20–21

When you experience God, the first stage you go through is the "forgive me, help me" stage. "Lord, I'm struggling with this. I can't stop doing this. Lord, forgive me. Lord, help me. Thank you, Lord—uh oh, Lord, I'm doing it again. Lord, help me. I'm sorry."

It's a frustrating and often defeating cycle.

But when I draw closer to my own Jesus, my vision sharpens, and I begin to realize, "There are other people everywhere. What in the world? Where have they been all my life?" All of the sudden people aren't road cones anymore. They have a pulse, just like I do. They hurt, just like I do. They fear, just like I do.

They long for that God-shaped void to be filled.

Just like I did.

This notion didn't hit home for me until I prepared a message on, of all things, evangelism. I intended to focus on the faith of the four men who brought their paralytic friend to Jesus in Mark 2. The house in Capernaum overflowed with people thronging around Jesus. Four guys climbed to the roof, tore a hole in it, and lowered their crippled friend to the floor in front of Jesus.

I planned to help launch a big evangelistic push, and this passage served as the pretext to a message designed to psych up everyone about evangelism. I'd always considered the persistence of the paralytic's friends a wonderful motivational tool for evangelism.

But something much simpler happens in the story. It isn't just about the four men getting their friend to Jesus; it's also about the one man who needed Jesus. Sometimes we focus more on our ministry than on the people we're ministering to. We talk about our ministry moments. We get all excited and learn witnessing outlines and tips on how to be bold.

But the closer we are to Jesus, the more we just see … individuals.

We draw close to Jesus, and he gives us our spiritual glasses. We start focusing on Jesus, and he starts focusing us on his purposes. We don't need to artificially excite people toward evangelism. The closer we get to Jesus, the more our eyes open to others around us. The

more we see as he sees, the more we act as he acted—
and acts—and we reach out to them.

After a youth camp, a young woman named Miriam
walked up to me. "Mark, I don't know what's happened,
but everything looks different to me," she said. "I go to
school and I see pain and all the hurts people are having. And then I see all these things I used to think were
cool, and they're not cool anymore."

She was wearing her God glasses. She could see her
life through God's eyes and discovered she needed to
change the way she lived. She received her real sight—
the eyesight of someone living for her own Jesus.

Your Own Walk

If you don't have your own walk with Jesus and you
hear a sermon encouraging you to share Jesus with others, the pastor's words will come to a fruitless end. But
if you see things as Jesus sees them, you won't be able
to stay silent.

Which begs the question: How do I get fitted for a
pair of those God-vision glasses?

The walk comes first. Trading a lifestyle of compromise for one of obedience will help you draw closer to
God. Close enough to see things as God does.

My friend Roger Glidewell of Global Youth Ministry showed me two interesting parallels from the Gospel of John. In chapter 13, Jesus reveals the difference his new covenant brings:

> "A new commandment I give to you, that you love one another: just as I have loved you, you also are to love one another. By this all people will know that you are my disciples, if you have love for one another."
>
> JOHN 13:34–35

Jesus gives us our first big teaching point: *When we love each other, the world will believe that we belong to Jesus.*

We cannot love the world before we demonstrate a lasting love for fellow believers. Loving fellow believers, especially ones you don't particularly care to hang with, is the only way to convince a lost world that he who lives inside us is real. We can write songs, stage revivals, and attend mega-rallies, but it's all banging gongs and clanging cymbals if not grounded in love for each other and carried out on behalf of God's purposes and glory.

Imagine a girl whose momma is sick and tired of the way her daughter is living. Momma throws her out on the side of the road on a Wednesday night. The girl wanders into a local church and slips into the back row at a youth event. Four girls walk up to her and want to know her. They introduce themselves, and the girl learns one is a cheerleader, one is a jock, one is a band student, and one is a Goth kid. Yet these four girls walk up together and ask her to sit with them during service because they're all friends. *That* would blow her mind.

And if that happened in my church, it would blow *my* mind. We could preach and I could sing and we could have a heavenly time, but if she walked in and saw people who aren't alike (in fact, who are very different) loving each other, she would know something at that church is different. Something is real.

The church has a long way to go before it is a faithful testimony to God's love in which there is no Jew or Greek, slave or free, male or female, but only brothers and sisters in Christ (Galatians 3:28).

Can you imagine eavesdropping on the first-century followers of Jesus? You'd have Peter saying, "Yeah, man, we were out there trying to catch something all last night. We went to our favorite hole and didn't get a nibble. We used every kind of lure and net we had. Nothing." Then Matthew the tax collector says, "Don't worry. Since it's so late in the year, you can just write off this loss. Just think of the fiscal ramifications on your budget."

Then Luke the physician pipes up. "Do you wash these nets when you're done? Do you understand what the seawater and bacteria are going to do to your pores?"

You have three guys from different backgrounds with various expertise and divergent interests. They have nothing in common. Nothing but Jesus. He alone is their common thread. You have a fisherman, a tax collector, and a doctor from different strata of society. They wouldn't have lunch together if you made them—and now these guys are best friends. How did that happen?

Jesus happened.

The world will change when the world sees that Christians love each other. There is nothing more effective for Christ's kingdom than this truth.

Now for Jesus' second big teaching point. This one nails me every time.

In John 17, Jesus prays to our heavenly Father before his arrest and crucifixion:

> "I do not ask for these only, but also for those who will believe in me through their word [*that's us, the church*], that they may all be one, just as you, Father, are in me,

and I in you, that they also may be in us,
so that the world may believe that you have
sent me."

JOHN 17:20–21 (note added)

When we love each other, the world will believe that Jesus belongs to God.

Lost people will believe Jesus is who he said he is, but only if we love each other. Jesus says it in his own prayer.

When we love each other, when we're one (just as Jesus prayed for us to be one), the consequences are amazing. Not only will the world see that we belong to Jesus, but it will realize that Jesus belongs to God. It will realize that Jesus *is* God. Lost people will begin to grasp the truth that our faith isn't just another religion but is different from anything they've ever witnessed. They'll see it's a fellowship — they'll see it's good news.

Why would they believe it's more than just religion and Jesus is more than all the other gods? Because these people who call themselves believers love each other. It's obvious they love each other. Nobody that different loves each other naturally. When we who have little in common demonstrate genuine love toward one another, heads turn. It's easier to believe we belong to Jesus. And it's easier to believe Jesus must be the answer because this Jesus truly is who he says he is.

He says he is the God of the universe.

He says he is the one true God you can call your own.

CHAPTER 6

A DIFFERENT KIND OF SONG

What This World Needs

What this world needs
Is not another sign-waving super saint that's better
  than you
Another ear-pleasing candy man afraid of the truth
Another prophet in an Armani suit

CAMERON "BLUE" RUSSELL LAY STARING AT THE featureless ceiling in his musty jail cell. He thought about his pregnant wife, replayed all his mistakes, and promised himself a better future. He had practiced religion his entire life. Now he was suffering a dose of the jailhouse kind.

Maybe this time he meant it.

The gun charge was old. He had been arrested for illegal possession of a firearm, sent to the wrong court, and set free pending trial. When the judge rerouted the case, it disappeared into one of the system's cracks. Even the occasional license check when the cops found him sleeping in yet another church parking lot uncovered nothing on the gun charge. He skated for two years, time he spent trying to piece together his fragmented life—until one day the police came calling again.

Blue's attempted suicide had propelled him out of the thug life. He escaped the gang, but his drug addiction kept him a homeless hustler. He pulled into church parking lots late at night to sleep in his car—the closest to a safe haven he knew, the closest to God his flesh let him get. Just enough Jesus to make it through the night. He could always grip the steering wheel and drive away, still in the sewer but still in control.

"I went to one church to sleep in the parking lot and somebody knocked on the window. He said, 'Could you not sleep in our parking lot? You're just making our church look bad.' I said, 'OK, I'm going to leave. I want you to know the reason I'm sleeping here is my parents are missionaries in Africa, and I don't have anything. I made some bad decisions, but this is why I'm here.' I could not find one Christian who would try and reach out," Blue said. "But I remember sleeping in the parking lot of Spivey Community Church, and it was the first place where somebody cared."

Billy Lord, the worship leader at Spivey, embraced the homeless teenager. Blue craved the acceptance, but he ran hot and cold, on fire for the Lord until the drug demons danced anew, and then he would slip and repent, sick of himself all over again. Through it all, Eveliina remained by his side. She stuck with him even after he cheated on her, even after the suicide attempt. Then she got pregnant, and Blue married her.

Two mouths to feed helped narrow Blue's path. He went to work and tried to settle down. They found an apartment. Eveliina was a month away from giving birth to Vanessa when the knock on the door came.

"Cameron Russell live here?"

The door opened, and the officer reached for his cuffs.

Bail was impossible. Blue was told he would have to wait out his court date behind bars—maybe two months, maybe six. Either way, he wouldn't be there for the birth of his baby.

But now at least somebody showed compassion. Pastor Roger from Spivey visited. "What do you want? What can I get for you?" the pastor asked.

"I need my Bible."

When night came, Blue stared at the ceiling and begged for sleep to serve his time for him. Now he owned yet another label: prisoner.

"I remember praying that night. I said, 'God, I hate my life, and I don't even want to get out of here because we're down and out on the other side. I need to know there is something for me on the other side of this wall, and I'll go. I'll do what you want me to do. I'm ready. I believe that you could open these doors and let me walk out, but I'm not asking for that. I deserve to be here, but I need some kind of confirmation. My faith is weak. I'm sorry to even ask for a sign, but can I have a sign please? If it's music, since I've always had an urging toward music, then let me know. If it's not, if you want me to go back to Africa and be a missionary with my parents, let me know. But I want to see the writing on the wall.'"

A few years earlier, Blue had tried to kill himself. Now he began to realize he needed a different kind of death. He needed to die to his old self.

The next morning, Blue wiped the sleep from his eyes and saw the same ceiling and the same four walls. But something caught his eye. Scratched into the bricks beside his bunk were six letters.

M-A-S-K-I-L.

In an instant, Blue knew that God had answered his prayer. An extensive background in music had taught Blue that *maskil* is Hebrew for "a different kind of song or one that requires great skill in its execution." Certain Bible translations refer to some psalms as *maskils*, or "contemplations," of David. Blue knew that an ancient sect of Hebrew scholars called themselves the *maskilim*, which meant "self-taught scholars." The word had stuck in Blue's mind when he discovered it years earlier.

"I thought, 'I'm seeing things, I'm crazy,'" Blue said. "I went to get this atheist in jail with me and said, 'You tell me if I'm crazy.' I told him what I prayed, and he looked at the wall and said, 'I don't know what you believe in, but that's real.' I said, 'I'll never turn back.'"

Now if he could just get out. Anguished at the thought of missing his daughter's birth in mere days, Blue gave Pastor Roger permission to tell the church of his arrest and incarceration. They held a nighttime prayer service for him.

The following morning, the intercom sounded in Blue's cell. "Get your stuff. You're going to court."

The judge slapped him with probation and time served, and Blue walked out of the jail and into the arms of his pregnant wife and the promise of a different kind of song.

A World in Need of Blue

Blue likes to come to our prayer room at Eagle's Landing and get on his knees. Sometimes he joins a few of his friends; sometimes he comes alone. We plead with God together. We fast together. He prays for my band.

I pray for the Bible study group he assembled to reach folks who are walking where he's been. He has wedged as many as thirty people into his living room to share this strange good news.

A 2006 visit to his family in Kenya somehow exorcised the anger that had been festering as his constant companion since boyhood. He is twenty-eight now, a product of the front lines of the mission field and the mean streets, one of the *maskilim* if one ever existed, self-taught to the hardest of hard cores.

"The biggest ministry I have right now is with people online through music. I had a kid write me the other day and say, 'I'm fifteen years old; I've been on coke for five months now, and I've lost everything. What do I do?' I got a chance to witness to the guy and just tell him straight up about Jesus," Blue said. "I had one guy online who heard some of the music and said, 'I'm so hopeless. How do I know Jesus?' I got to disciple him online, and this guy is in Austria. He got saved, and now he's doing his thing over there."

One of Blue's coworkers, Tim, denied God's existence. Then tragedy struck. Tim couldn't hide his devastation at the news that his little boy was suffering from a life-threatening intestinal disorder. Doctors ruled it incurable. The atheist turned to the only man of faith he knew.

Blue prayed in specifics with Tim: *God, heal this child. Do it so Tim will know you're real. Show yourself to be the mighty God you are.*

The very next day, Tim walked up to Blue and wanted to know about this God who had just healed his child. Puzzled doctors had sent the boy home earlier in the day, wondering what had happened in between the old tests and the new.

Blue explained to Tim what happens between the old and the new.

Right there at work, Tim asked Jesus to forgive his sins and to be his Lord. Blue's father, Shayne Russell, visited from Africa and baptized Tim during our 2008 Easter service, the same day in which Blue's seven-minute videotaped testimony played to more than three thousand people. They heard about the missionary kid whose fade was as slow and willful as his climb to restoration. They learned how he uses his story to sling a lifeline to crackheads and drug dealers, and how he unveils the beautiful steps laid out in Peter's second letter:

> But also for this very reason, giving all diligence, add to your faith virtue, to virtue knowledge, to knowledge self-control, to self-control perseverance, to perseverance godliness, to godliness brotherly kindness,

and to brotherly kindness love. For if these things are yours and abound, you will be neither barren nor unfruitful in the knowledge of our Lord Jesus Christ. For he who lacks these things is shortsighted, even to blindness, and has forgotten that he was cleansed from his old sins.

2 PETER 1:5–9 NKJV

"Shortsighted, even to blindness"—remember the God glasses?

"You start with faith," Blue said. "You have that faith, but you're not going to be a biblical scholar. You're not going to understand the Bible at first, but it doesn't take that to do good deeds. So in the name of Jesus do good things. Then comes virtue, and it starts to build. On top of virtue add knowledge. Get in the Word and start to understand it, and as that knowledge grows, start to learn some self-control. You're not going to kick crack, you're probably not going to kick lust. Life is tough. But I think the people who fail are the ones who say, 'I'm a Christian, I'm going to do this! Yeah! I'm ready to serve God!' And then, boom, they fail, and the bottom falls out: *'What happened, Jesus? Why did you leave me?'* Well, if we're realistic, after the slow fade there has to be a slow climb as well.

"I heard someone say, 'You know if you're a Christian by how quickly you run to repentance after you sin.' You might sin, but start learning self-control. Eventually self-control will turn into perseverance, and perseverance turns into godliness, where we can actually get up in the morning and live just for God's will, just to be like him. And only then will we truly understand brotherly kindness, only then can we truly be kind to other people we don't like out there. And then comes love. Christ is love. So for me and for some of the other guys in our Bible study group, this outlined the slow climb after the slow fade."

Blue brings Eveliina and his three little girls to worship with us each Sunday. He's easy to spot, but not just because of his hair, tattoos, and earrings. He sits somewhere in the first few rows of the same section every week. It's the section directly in front of our worship leader, with whom I lead singing on Sunday mornings. His name is Billy Lord, the same music leader who embraced Blue at Spivey Community Church more than a decade ago.

"I'm excited," Blue said. "I know tomorrow will have its failures. I know the more I seek, the more I will find. I know the descent into sin is so endless, but I also know the climb to knowing and having a personal relationship with Jesus is endless. I can climb as high as

I want from here until the day I die, and that's based on my diligence and my obedience to his calling. And that goes for every single one of us in this life. If we go to church on Sunday and only sit there and then wonder why we get nothing out of it, that's why. I had to do something to drive myself into sin. I also think driving toward godliness requires something. There's action. There has to be action."

Blue Russell has carried labels his entire life, most of them bad. Now the only ones important to him are printed in neat ink on his body. On the right side of his neck the name Eveliina is scripted, on the left the name Vanessa, his firstborn. The inside of his forearms, just above the tattooed nails in his wrist, feature words in Old English letters descending from the elbows. The left forearm reminds him of his earthly home. It reads FAMILY.

The right forearm reminds him of the night a twelve-year-old saw the promises of Psalm 91 become reality on the violent streets of Goma, Zaire. And it reminds him of his heavenly home and what he's supposed to do until he gets there, something that requires much skill in its execution, something that takes him back to the day he saw the writing on the wall.

His right forearm reads MASKIL.

God's Mysterious Grace

Driving down the interstate in downtown Atlanta one day, I almost swerved into another lane when my eyes fixated on a mammoth billboard. It read: *Saturday is the Lord's Day. Sunday is the Mark of the Beast.*

At first the words shocked me, and then I got mad. Then I got hurt, and then I got mad again. I mumbled to myself, "How much money are they paying for that sign, and this is their shot? This is their opportunity to speak to the world, and *this* is what they had to say? You've got to be kidding."

The sign appeared to be the work of an error-filled group that believes salvation is based on works, such as keeping the Sabbath. While the sign is an example of false teaching, it reminded me of how far we humans will go to inject ourselves and our ideas into the gospel.

Even the church, the body of Christ, can sometimes hinder rather than help God's program for humanity. Our churches may not pay thousands of dollars for heretical billboards, but we do struggle with our own issues.

Blue's life story is an instance of God's mysterious grace in all its messiness, an example of God rescuing and using someone the world would have considered unfit. Blue's story also reminds us that God is a God of balance. The Bible as a whole is a portrait of the one true God, a God of justice and mercy, truth and grace. It is a portrait of Jesus. He is what this world needs. He is what every individual needs. One heart at a time discovering Jesus.

John, called the disciple whom Jesus loved, confirms the source of this balance: "For the law was given through Moses; *grace* and *truth* came through Jesus Christ" (John 1:17, emphasis added).

Jesus is the source of perfect balance. To walk with your own Jesus is to walk in balance. A person who is out of balance is a person who could be walking more closely with Jesus—and the same goes for churches.

Even in the Old Testament, long before Jesus shed his blood to bring the New Covenant of salvation by grace through faith in him, God's balance is depicted. The book of Psalms reveals at several points (25:10; 57:3; 61:7; 115:1) that the Lord exists and acts in *mercy* and *truth*, as translated in the King James and New King James Versions. Other versions refer to God's "loving-kindness and truth" or "love and faithfulness."

God is never incomplete, never lacks anything, and never acts out of anything but perfect balance. Within the span of five psalms (from 85:10 to 89:14) three different psalmists characterize God as exhibiting mercy and truth.

He loves and he judges (mercy and truth), and the two are not mutually exclusive. In fact, they are interdependent. Sometimes what we see as a harsh judgment is nothing more than an unfathomable grace we may never understand in this life. God is a God of balance, and it is reassuring to rest in this truth: "But You, O Lord, are a God full of compassion, and gracious, longsuffering and abundant in mercy and truth" (Psalm 86:15 NKJV).

Psalm 25 goes a step further and puts God's mercy and truth into action through the church: "All the paths of the LORD are mercy and truth, to such as keep His covenant and His testimonies" (Psalm 25:10 NKJV). In other words, God intends for the believer to reflect him and live in mercy and truth, that is, to live in balance.

We get all out of whack sometimes, trumpeting our favorite verses until our tongues hang out. We strap ourselves to the gospel. Jesus is the only way to God, but sometimes we act as if *we're* the only way to Jesus. Our goal is to live a life of scriptural balance that pleases the Lord and never gets in his way.

Little Boxes, Big Boxes

I helped lead a group from our church on a mission trip and tour of Israel a few years ago. A friend named Yoni guided us. He teaches at Hebrew University, and he's been our tour guide on four trips I've taken to Israel. He used a line from the Mishnah, the oral law of Judaism, which gave instruction for men to "make a fence round the Torah." Christians know the Torah as Genesis, Exodus, Leviticus, Numbers, and Deuteronomy, or the Pentateuch. It contains the written law, the Ten Commandments.

In Judaism, adding oral traditions (the fence) has been a way to ensure that people do not violate the written law by keeping them further away from the original commandments.

Even Jesus invoked the rabbinic teaching method of fence building. Yoni explained Jesus' teaching by drawing a small square and pointing to it as he quoted Jesus: "You've heard it said, 'Do not kill.'" Then Yoni drew a larger square around the smaller one, pointed to it, and said, "But I say to you that if you hate your brother, you've committed murder in your heart."

With the larger square surrounding the smaller one, he had added a fence around the requirement. The idea is to step back from the written law so as to not even come close to violating it. Jesus, like those who followed such Jewish traditions as fence building, understood this as a tool to help a person avoid sin — but he *also* taught this way to show the impossibility of perfection and the necessity of a Savior.

Small box: "You've heard it said, 'Do not commit adultery.'"

Larger box: "But I tell you that if you look at a woman with lust, you've committed adultery in your heart."

Jesus knew fence building. His fences weren't intended to ultimately frustrate people but to lead people to him. His unattainable demands must have blown the minds of even the strictest scholars, who were legalists but nevertheless literalists. At least people found it *possible* to do what they instructed. A man could succeed at never committing adultery — but *not* at never looking at a woman lustfully.

When God gave Moses the Ten Commandments (which Galatians calls "our tutor," or "guardian," pointing us to Christ because we can't obey them), he instructed people to "remember the Sabbath day, to keep it holy" (Exodus 20:8).

The Israelites eventually engaged their teachers in this kind of dialogue:

"So how do you remember the Sabbath day, to keep it holy? How do you rest on the Sabbath?"

"Well, let's see. We probably shouldn't work."

Check. That's one. "OK, what constitutes work?"

"Hmmm. Let's see, you can't lift this or plow this."

Check. Got it. "What else?"

You can see that such a thought process leads to fences around fences around fences, soon obscuring not only the original law but even some of the very activities that make us human.

The absurdity touched even Jesus. The Pharisees yelled at him when his disciples picked grain to eat on the Sabbath (Mark 2:24). Staying outside a man-made fence was, for these religious leaders, more important than staying nourished. But Jesus set them straight, pointing out that the Sabbath was made for *us*, and not the other way around.

Instead of realizing God sees the heart and gauges our thoughts and motives, we often get hung up on externals. Too often, today's church is filled with bad fence builders. Let me give you an example:

> "Don't dance."
>
> "Don't dance? What do you mean, 'Don't dance'?"
>
> "Well, dancing is a sin."
>
> "Where in the world are you getting that from? Biblical heroes of our faith danced. David danced so hard that he humiliated his overly proud wife!"
>
> "Well, that's different ..."

I'm sure you can fill in the rest of the conversation, and supply a bunch of your own examples—some funny, and some bordering on the tragic.

The point is this: It is wrong to say that *no* Christian may dance, and it is wrong to say that *all* Christians *must* dance. Remember, God looks at our hearts, at our motives.

So if we're thinking about dancing, for example, we should know that, within his culture, David danced as an expression of a heart overflowing with worship and gratitude to the Lord. Today's pop culture has nothing to do with being enraptured by the love of a holy God. Since the Bible clearly warns Christians to flee sexual immorality (1 Corinthians 6:18), we need to be careful with our involvement in certain activities at certain places. We need to ask ourselves what would be the wise thing to do. We need to guard our hearts, whether we're sitting still or wanting to boogie down.

The worst approach is to build a bad fence by declaring absolutely that dancing (or something else) is a sin. Certain forms of dancing are clearly sinful—and certain forms are clearly not. Instead of building a bad fence, we need to learn the biblical truth in its context and in love explain the wisest course.

Too often, believers teach truth but fence it with human traditions. Jesus railed against this approach. He reserved his harshest criticism for religious elitists who concerned themselves with ritual and pretense when inside they were dead and decaying. What good is it, he asked, to keep the letter of a human law that destroys the spirit of God's law?

God lacks nothing. We cannot add a thing to God or to his message. He and his Word are complete. I pray that we would stop teaching a "Jesus-plus" theology. I'm the first to admit the temptation to add our pet issues or convictions to "Jesus alone." However, the words of Ephesians 2:8−9 call us to live in humility and total reliance on God: "For by grace you have been saved through faith. And this is not your own doing; it is the gift of God, not a result of works, so that no one may boast."

Out of Balance

Paul wrote to believers in Galatia to combat the Judaizers, false teachers who mixed a professed belief in Jesus with the external rituals of Orthodox Judaism. They wanted to keep the new wine of Jesus' gospel in old wineskins, which Jesus himself repudiated (Matthew 9:17). The Judaizers erected bad fences. They added to the gospel by saying, "Yeah, you have to be saved by believing in Jesus, but you *also* have to be circumcised and offer these sacrifices and observe this New Moon festival. Oh, and you can't eat this food over here …" They had a Jesus-plus theology. Perhaps some had good intentions, but they built fences around the gospel so high that the good news was hidden.

Before Christ, the Jewish teachers took the Ten Commandments and transformed them into more than six hundred laws. Galatians reveals a recurrence of this legalistic obsession in the early church. Judaizers had a knee-jerk reaction to the excessive liberties flaunted by some of the new grace-filled Christians. Believers always should be wary of abusing freedom in Christ, but the Judaizers in Galatia mimicked their forefathers and weighted God's Word with their personal likes and dislikes.

When I look at the American church today, I see denominations emerging from differences of opinion on nonessentials in Scripture. For many people, evangelical denominations are little more than comfort zones. We need to be careful—and I'm holding up a mirror here—to communicate that the gospel is paramount; our issues and tastes are secondary. God is a God of mercy and truth. He is a God of balance. Too often I see fingers pointed behind harsh words: "You people are gay and you need to be fixed. You're a welfare crackhead and you need to repent." We can tell people of their need for Jesus in a sensible and sensitive way: "You're hurt, just like I am. Let me tell you about somebody who loves you and wants the best for you."

I'm not more holy than you because I have a fish sticker on my car or because my hair is shorter than yours. At the same time, we shouldn't assume that wallowing in the slop like Mr. Every Man somehow makes God appealing to the unbeliever we're trying to reach or endears us to God, as if the holiest of holies is impressed with our aptitude for all things human. God is not impressed with humanity. God is impressed with one person. Himself. There is nothing God wants glorified or seeks to spotlight more than himself. And that's OK. He's God.

Since God made us in his image to glorify him, our job is to be a reflection of that spotlight. What this world needs is for us to stop hiding behind our relevance, blending in so well that people can't see the difference. The difference is what sets the world free.

To grow into Christlikeness is to grow into mercy and truth. Micah 6:8 (NKJV) asks what God requires of us and then provides the answer: "to do justly, to love mercy, and to walk humbly with your God."

We strike this balance by pursuing our own Jesus through obedience in Bible study, prayer, worship, serving, and witnessing. We do this through our own Jesus and for our own Jesus because Jesus alone is God, because he alone is worthy, and because what this world needs is ...

> a Savior who will rescue,
> a Spirit who will lead,
> a Father who will love them
> in their time of need.

More than anything, that's what this world needs. And the only people who will lead the world to the one true God are those who, like my friend Blue, respond to his gentle, ever-present call for the personal.

Your own Jesus insists on it.

"The problem with Christianity is that we can make it a religion," Blue said. "We put it on our Facebook page, and we say, 'I'm a Christian' and go to church on Sunday, and that's it. We sit in the pew and warm it up and leave and say, 'That was a great service. The Holy Spirit was moving there.' We go eat some Mexican food and go home and forget about it while we are at work the next week. Faith without works is dead. Why talk about this if we're not going to live it?

"If I spend so much time looking behind me to count the distance between where I'm at and where I was, I'm going to end up finding myself back where I was. For me, everything back there is so heavy that I prefer not to go back. I keep my eyes on the goal and move forward," Blue said. "Honestly, I don't know what tomorrow will bring. I don't want to know. But I know Jesus will be there. And if I'm still here, I'll be seeking him."

CONCLUSION

SAY IT OUT LOUD

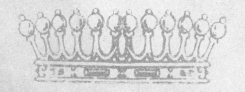

ERIC TIMMS IS AN ARTIST WHO PAINTS PICTURES while he talks about Jesus. I watched him paint once, and his canvas didn't resemble a portrait at all. It looked like a bunch of shapes slapped together. It looked, frankly, like a mess. Eric talked the whole time he painted, and I wondered if his message was getting in the way of his art.

Then, as he concluded his message, he spun the giant frame upside down, and—boom!—an amazing portrait of a compassionate Jesus jumped off the canvas. It took my breath away.

"If you don't see Jesus for who he is and your picture of Jesus is that he's judgmental and in your face, then someone painted you the wrong picture of Jesus," Eric said. "If you see this kind of Jesus or that kind of Jesus and you've attached to him all these labels we've always heard, then it's because somebody painted you the wrong Jesus."

What kind of Jesus is your life painting?

The look of your painting will have a lot to do with where you are within the cycle. Are you mired somewhere in the downward cycle of compromise? Or are you climbing the upward road of growth?

In John 8:31–32, Jesus tells a group of new believers how they can know they are growing in him: "If you abide in my word, you are truly my disciples, and you will know the truth, and the truth will set you free." He connects one prerequisite to being his disciple— continuing in his Word. To be a disciple of Christ is to be a lifelong learner, to pursue him in order to experience him. That's what the Greek word for *disciple* means.

Are you pursuing Jesus? Do you really know him? You can agree with the Bible's claims about Jesus and still not belong to him. You have to know him in the sense of trusting him for your life here and now and for eternity. It's the *pisteuo* kind of belief—weight-bearing belief rather than mental assent to certain facts.

Sometimes it seems we believe that since Jesus isn't

physically present, we have to hold on to *things* instead. Jesus can become a book instead of a person.

But the One who created the world isn't a Christian bestseller. He's not a habit, an idea, a lifestyle, or a set of rules. He's not a daily routine or an obstacle course.

Jesus is a person.

Stop and concentrate for a moment. Try to block everything else out. Ready?

Be honest and ask yourself this question: Is Jesus a real, living, glorified person to you? Is Jesus real in every sense, more real than any real thing you've ever encountered, so real that the word *real* fails in its meager efforts to describe . . .

our true, loving, eternal Deity

God with us

Almighty Immanuel

the Maker of the ground underneath you, the sky above you, the air you breathe, the lungs that breathe it, and the life you live

our Redeemer

Life-giver

Sustainer

Guide

Comforter

and Friend?

His name is Jesus.

Say it out loud: *His name is Jesus.*
He is the one, true God.
God come in the flesh,
God crucified,
God resurrected,
God glorified,
God reigning on high.
And yet he desires a relationship with all and conde-scends to lift us out of the pit.

Is he your Savior? Is he your Lord? Your *Master*?
Is he your very own Jesus?

THANK YOU

THIS BOOK WOULD STILL BE A JUMBLED BALL ricocheting around my noggin without the help of so many wonderful friends. I hope I won't forget anyone, but I'm especially grateful to the following folks for helping me pull this off:

Jesus: You, of course, come first. If I didn't know you for my own and enjoy our friendship, I'd have nothing. I love you, Lord, but I know it's because you loved me first.

Melanie, my wife, and my mom and dad: You are always instrumental in everything I do. Your support and love keep my tank full, no matter how often Atlanta runs out of gas.

Norman Miller, Mike Jay, and everyone at Proper Management: Thank you for your leadership and most of all for your friendship.

Byron Williamson: Thank you for your incredible

guidance, creativity, and patience in developing the ideas behind this book. And thank you for working so hard with the great folks at Zondervan to send out a very dear message from my heart to the world.

Tim Luke: Thank you for doing everything short of duct taping me to a chair to get all of this out of my head. You are a great partner and a true friend.

Angela Scheff: Thank you for making us look better than we should. You're a great editor.

The students at Eagle's Landing First Baptist Church, my ELFBC church family, and my band, Casting Crowns: I love you all and thank you for always refreshing me and inspiring me.

Pastor Tim Dowdy: Thanks for the freedom. You're the best because you get it. You really get it.

Reagan Farris and Georgia Sexton: I'm glad I have you. I'm glad we all have Jesus.

Cameron "Blue" Russell, Eveliina Russell, Miriam Foster, Michael Learner (you know who you are), Barry Riner (and so do you), Eric Timms (*www.nooneunderground.com*), Tony Nolan (*www.tonynolan.org*), Roger Glidewell (*www.globalyouthministry.com*), and Candace: I appreciate your willingness to tell your stories, share your lives, and be my friends. You made this book worth the effort. I hope you inspire others as you have inspired me.

Love 'em like Jesus . . .

MARK HALL

DISCUSSION GUIDE

This guide can be used for personal reflection or group study and includes two sections for each chapter. The first section, titled "Through the Door," features questions to facilitate self-examination or discussion with others. The second section, titled "Cycle Breakers" for the first three chapters and "Cycle Makers" for the last three chapters, includes pointers to help emerge from the cycle of compromise and move toward restoration and growth.

Chapter 1
Explaining the Wind

Through the Door

1. Have you accepted God's forgiveness and his pledge that he has removed your sin as far as the east is from the west? If so, when did you grasp this revelation? What did it mean to you then? What does it mean to you now? What has resulted from your knowing this to be true? If you have been unable to accept it as truth, search your heart before answering this: What is keeping you from trusting that pledge?

2. Do you have any compartments you're keeping for yourself and hiding from the Lord? What are they?

3. Second Corinthians 5:21 (NKJV) states, "For He made Him who knew no sin to be sin for us, that we might become the righteousness of God in Him." In light of this verse, where is your walk with Jesus? Are you displaying the righteousness of Christ? How have you grown in righteousness? In which areas do you need to improve?

Cycle Breakers

1. Hold aloft the Word of God to every area of your life and ask God to dissolve any compartments you may have.

2. Identify strongholds (pursuits and interests that are extremely difficult to surrender to the Lord) and pray and fast over those areas. Make a list and check up on yourself.

3. Ask yourself, "What does God's Word say about this?"

4. Just do it. Walking with your own Jesus isn't mystical—sometimes it's as simple as the act of will (the volition) it takes to turn off the television and open your Bible.

CHAPTER 2
Infinite

Through the Door

1. Describe a time when you found yourself at a place you never thought you'd be, doing things you never thought you'd do. What triggered your downward spiral and what sustained it? Try to put into words how you felt and what you thought, and what your outlook on the future was.

2. Identify a time when you sinned and brought someone else down with you. How did it make you feel to hurt someone else? How did it impact your relationship with that person, and how is your relationship with that person now? Did the impact last, or has there been healing? Do you still need to reconcile?

3. This is going to take extraordinary courage and transparency. Take a moment to pray and ask God to pinpoint any area in which you are making compromises, however small, that could lead to something more damaging. Be honest before God and remember your answer as a commitment to the

Lord to seek his will and obey him to rid your life of compromising choices and actions. If you journal, write down this specific area of compromise, or write it somewhere in your Bible or in the margin of this page. If it is too embarrassing to write specifics, then refer to it as "my sin."

4. The wonderful news is that the person who delights in the Lord Jesus and meditates on his Word has abundant life. There is hope, even at our lowest point. God makes sure we understand that the slow fade can be followed by resurrection. Read Psalm 1, paying particular attention to verses 2 – 3, then consider what this promise means to you. You may want to record your answer and today's date somewhere and ask the Lord to help you realize his promise.

Cycle Breakers

1. Read Psalm 1 and determine where you are. Are you delighting, walking, standing, or sitting?

2. When you know what you're doing is wrong, however small, think of what even that tiny sin cost Jesus.

3. Avoid any environment or counsel that brings temptation, especially in your weak areas.

4. Tell God you're sorry. And mean it.

5. Turn and walk the other way.

CHAPTER 3

Stuck

Through the Door

1. Contemplate what you know to be true about God: his Person, power, provision, sovereignty. Compare these truths to *how your life reveals* what you believe about God. What do your actions say you believe about him versus what Scripture says about him?

2. Think about your spiritual gifts. How do they shape how you see God and his role in the affairs of human beings? Now think about your closest friend or relative and his or her spiritual gifts. Name some of the obvious differences in the ways the two of you view and respond to God based on your spiritual gifts.

3. If you could have the god you want, what would he look like? Now compare that god to the God who is. What are the differences, and in what areas do you need to ask God's direction for change?

4. How do you see God's presence and power at work right now?

5. What distractions cloud your spiritual growth and perception and stunt God's transforming work in you?

6. Do you remember the last time you felt pierced by the Holy Spirit about something God wanted to correct in you? Think back to your response and the results.

Cycle Breakers

1. Note the differences between the god you want and the God who is.

2. Seek to look like Jesus instead of making God look like you.

3. Return to your first love. Jesus says be zealous and repent.

4. Pray over your walk with Jesus; ask him to speak to you as you read his Word.

5. Identify your disconnects. What is causing the difference between you at the altar and you outside the door?

6. Obey the Holy Spirit, no matter how large or small his directive. Sell out!

7. Find a mature Christian to serve as your mentor and accountability partner. Get over your fears and open your life.

Chapter 4

Newness

Through the Door

1. Can you identify the instant when the Word of God first came alive to you? Think back to that time and reflect on how God moved in your heart. How did you respond or fail to respond, and what were the results?

2. Psalm 119:105 states that God's Word is a lamp to our feet and a light to our path. In what ways has God's Word illuminated your life and impacted its direction? Conversely, identify a few times when you failed to obey God's Word. What were the circumstances, your actions, and the results? What did you learn?

3. Since Scripture is the power of God for salvation (Romans 1:16), why do you think so many of us believers struggle with simply sharing Scripture with the lost? Since God uses the power of Scripture to save, are we exhibiting unbelief when we refuse to share it?

4. Romans 12:2 tells us not to be conformed to this
   world but to be transformed by the renewal of our
   minds. What are your personal study habits in
   God's Word? Is it a vital part of your day? If not,
   are you willing to make a commitment to develop a
   systematic, daily Bible study regimen?

5. When did you last intentionally place someone
   ahead of yourself and submit to his or her wishes
   even though you preferred something else? Reflect
   on how you felt at the moment you decided to
   subjugate yourself, and how you felt afterward.

6. When did you last confront someone over his or
   her unscriptural choices or actions? In hindsight,
   did you handle it properly? What would you do
   differently, if anything?

7. Do you need to be reconciled to anyone? Are you
   willing to obey Jesus and take the first step by
   reaching out to the person who holds something
   against you? Write down that person's name, the
   situation, and how you plan to work toward a
   reconciliation this week.

Cycle Makers

1. Turn from apathy and start turning pages.

2. Don't turn pages too fast. Soak in God's Word.

3. Have a conversation with God while you read. Listen more than you speak. Ask God to show you something new in his Word today.

4. Learn Scriptures to bolster you against your weak spots and potential areas of compromise.

5. Love God by showing him to someone who doesn't know him today. A gentle kindness in his name can last an eternity.

6. Resolve to submit to someone else's wishes today, even if you disagree.

7. Pray for a friend or loved one who is living outside of God's will today. Begin asking the Lord whether he has a role for you. And then be patient. When you think you're ready to talk to that person, stop and pray some more.

CHAPTER 5
The Roman Son

Through the Door

1. What do you think the world sees when it looks at the church? List positive aspects first, then list some areas in which the church should improve.

2. Are you a member of a local church? If not, why not? Since Jesus himself established the church (Matthew 16:18), be honest with yourself and explain your rationale behind not joining a local church.

3. If you are a member of a local church, what are some ways members are reaching out to each other within the church? You may have to talk with a staff member to get details, but this exercise will help educate you on the life of your church and whether it is fulfilling its Great Commission role. (If it's not, be assured it's OK to find a church that obeys Jesus.)

4. If you are a member of a local church, list some ways your church is reaching out to Every Man. Again, you may need to get details from a staff member. Don't be embarrassed if you don't know. Everyone is uninformed at some point and has to start somewhere.

5. As you reflect on your walk with the Lord, in what areas should you prayerfully seek to improve in serving and loving others both inside and outside the church?

Cycle Makers

1. Is there someone you need to forgive and extend a clean slate? God says do it.

2. Find the most unlovable person in your life and do something in love for him or her. If you do it for that person, you do it for Jesus.

3. Identify a believer who could use a helping hand and extend it this week.

4. Walk up to Mr. or Ms. Every Man and extend the love of Jesus in a tangible way this week.

CHAPTER 6
A Different Kind of Song

Through the Door

1. What does it mean to you that believers often attach their own issues and traditions to the gospel? Can you remember an instance in which you or someone you know erred by using a "Jesus-plus" theology? Explain.

2. In what ways do you need to become more balanced between mercy and truth?

3. Do you know anyone like Blue? How have you responded to that person? Have you been balanced? No one is too far gone for God to reach, but have your actions — or inactions — suggested you truly believe this? In what ways?

Cycle Makers

1. Read the Scriptures about balance, learn their context and truth, and apply them.

2. Die to irrelevant personal tastes and love another believer or reach a lost person.

3. Erase your man-made fences.

CONCLUSION
Say It Out Loud

Through the Door

1. Try to look at your life from a lost person's perspective. If an unsaved person described the portrait of Jesus you have painted, what would the portrait look like at home? At work? At church?

2. If the portraits you described do not depict a biblical Jesus in all three places, explain why they don't. Also, explain what steps you need to take to paint a more accurate picture of our Savior.

3. Looking back over this book, what does it mean to you to have "your own Jesus"? How do you intend to make Jesus more your own? In other words, how will you pursue a closer fellowship with Jesus? If you are so led, record at least three commitments toward this end and then sign and date it underneath.

Cycle Makers

1. Show the world an accurate portrait of Jesus today.

PERMISSION NOTICES

Chapter 1: Explaining the Wind

"East to West" (Mark Hall, Bernie Herms): Copyright © 2007 Club Zoo Music (BMI) SWECS Music (BMI) My Refuge Music (BMI) (adm. by EMI CMG Publishing) / Word Music (ASCAP) / Banahama Tunes (ASCAP). All rights reserved. Used by permission.

Chapter 2: Infinite

"Slow Fade" (Mark Hall): Copyright © 2007 Club Zoo Music (BMI) SWECS Music (BMI) My Refuge Music (BMI) (adm. by EMI CMG Publishing). All rights reserved. Used by permission.

Chapter 3: Stuck

"Somewhere in the Middle" (Mark Hall): Copyright © 2007 Club Zoo Music (BMI) SWECS Music (BMI) My Refuge Music (BMI) (adm. by EMI CMG Publishing). All rights reserved. Used by permission.

Chapter 4: Newness

"The Word Is Alive" (Mark Hall, Steven Curtis Chapman): Copyright © 2007 Sparrow Song (BMI) Club Zoo Music (BMI) SWECS Music (BMI) My Refuge Music (BMI) Peach Hill Songs (BMI) (adm. by EMI CMG Publishing). All rights reserved. Used by permission.

Chapter 5: The Roman Son

"Every Man" (Mark Hall, Bernie Herms, Nichole Nordeman): Copyright © 2007 Birdwing Music (ASCAP) Club Zoo Music (BMI) SWECS Music (BMI) Birdboy Songs (ASCAP) My Refuge Music (BMI) (adm. by EMI CMG Publishing) / Word Music (ASCAP) / Banahama Tunes (ASCAP). All rights reserved. Used by permission.

Chapter 6: A Different Kind of Song

"What This World Needs" (Mark Hall, Hector Cervantes): Copyright © 2007 Club Zoo Music (BMI) SWECS Music (BMI) My Refuge Music (BMI) Land of the Giants Music (BMI) (adm. by EMI CMG Publishing). All rights reserved. Used by permission.

Complete Your Casting Crowns Collection!

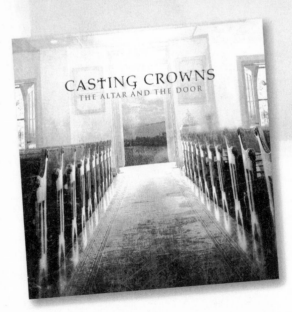

Casting Crowns
The Altar and The Door

Includes:
· East to West,
· Every Man
· Slow Fade

Casting Crowns
Lifesong

Includes:
· Praise You In
  This Storm
· Lifesong
· Does Anybody
  Hear Her

Casting Crowns
Casting Crowns

Includes:
· Voice of Truth
· Who Am I
· If We Are The
  Body

Look for Casting Crowns New CD
Releasing Fall 2009!

For more information, visit www.CastingCrowns.com